COLORED GLASS

COLORED GLASS

Derek C. Davis &
Keith Middlemas

photographs by
Michael Plomer

Clarkson N. Potter, Inc.

Publisher NEW YORK

Produced by Design Yearbook Limited, 21 Ivor Place, London N.W.1.
Published by Clarkson N. Potter, Inc., 419 Park Avenue South, New York, N.Y. 10016.
Text set by Yendall & Company Limited, Riscatype House, 22/25 Red Lion Court, Fleet Street, London E.C.4.
Colour origination by Supreme Litho Limited, 77/79 Parkway, Camden Town, London N.W.1.
Printed by L. Van Leer & Company N.V. of Amsterdam.
Bound by Nevett, Key & Whiting Limited, The Hyde, Colindale, London N.W.9.

Art Director: Ian Cameron.
House Editor and Designer: Tom Carter.

Printed in Holland and bound in England.

Library of Congress Catalog Card No. 68-31839

Photographs by Michael Plomer, with the exception of those for pages 46 (lower), 47 (lower), 57, 58, 63 (lower), 64, 83, 84, 85 (upper), 88, 89, 90, 97, 98, 99, 101 (left), 107 (lower).

CONTENTS

We are greatly indebted to the following private collectors, museums and antique dealers who have very kindly allowed us to take photographs of specimen glasses in their possession:

Mr and Mrs K. A. Alexander

Corning Museum of Glass, New York

Mr Geoffrey Godden

Godden of Worthing Limited

J. Haslim Limited

Mr E. M. Hutchinson

Mr J. G. Littledale

Mr and Mrs A. L. Middleton

Miss H. R. Morris

Mrs Laura Seddon

Mr P. de Wesselow

Worthing Museum

The Hon. Mrs R. J. P. Wyatt and
Mr O. Wyatt

We are also most grateful to those authors who have given permission to quote the passages which appear in the text.

Introduction

The best known and most often quoted account of the origin of glass-making is that of Pliny the Elder, the Roman encyclopaedist, writing about A.D. 30, 2,000 years after the event, of the Phoenician merchants camping near a river in Syria who used some of their ship's cargo of natron to support their cooking pots. This 'accidental' interpretation has been adopted by many recognised authorities, from Apsley Pellatt in *The Curiosities of Glass Making*, published in 1849, to present day authors. Accidental discovery was at least a possibility and it illustrates the fundamental requirements of the first glass workers: natron (a variety of soda), sand and heat.

Apsley Pellatt, who was well known as a lecturer and maker of cameo portraits in glass, stated, 'The Art of Making Glass is reputed to have been discovered by accident. This inference is strengthened by the fact that it is scarcely possible to excite a fire of sufficient heat for metallurgical operation without vitrifying part of the bricks or stones of the furnace. Of such imperfect vitrification, the "Glass" occasionally dug up on the sites of buildings destroyed by great conflagrations, is a specimen.'

There is little doubt that glass-making originated in Egypt and fragments found in Egyptian tombs at Thebes show an amazing variety of techniques and colours; illustrating how rapidly the early craftsmen mastered not only the art of making vessels of glass but also of decorating them and making them attractive by an astonishing diversity of designs and patterns. The brilliance, as well as the variety, of colours on every piece is remarkable. Many such articles can be seen in museums and private collections today.

The majority of the beads which ornamented mummies, referred to by many writers as early evidence of Egyptian glass-making, were not entirely glass but were composed of burnt clay or earthenware covered with a glaze. As early as 3500 B.C. the Egyptians also used tiles made from a clay-sand mixture covered with a blue copper glaze. Pictures on the walls of tombs from the Theban period (3000 to 1700 B.C.) have been revealed, illustrating scenes from the lives of Egyptian potters. Methods of modelling vases by hand and then firing them in ovens can be seen. In pyramids of this period the earliest examples of glazed earthenware were discovered. Here, then, lies the link between the use of glaze by the Egyptian potters and the accidental discovery of glass.

'Thus we meet the potter in the semi-darkness of pre-dynastic Egypt as the initiator of the art of glass-making; it was the potter who improved his roughly kneaded, and imperfectly turned, porous articles by dipping them into a glaze. This advance was certainly unintentional; it arose from the craftsman's urge to improve his articles by this trick. Such "improvements" existed in every craft and in glass-making they were frequently of decisive significance. Let us picture this lucky accident; the clay which that prehistoric "inventor" placed on his wheel, perhaps came, for lack of better, from the banks of an inland lake, that contained salts or potash, such as there are thousands along the North African coast. Perhaps it contained also quartz sands as well as soda, perhaps even lime and potash salt which form a high percentage in those lakes. Such raw materials, when melted in the fire, became—unintentionally and accidentally—glass.'[1]

Egyptian craftsmen quickly and skilfully took advantage of the natural and suitable minerals of their locality and this new and mysterious material took its place amongst the domestic and decorative arts.

Protected by the security of Egypt from war or interference, with an abundant supply of the basic ingredients—silica, in the form of sand; soda, the necessary alkali, from the natron lakes; and acacia groves to provide the fuel for heating—glass manufacture was able to develop. The glaze used on clay figures and heads and all forms of pottery could be opaque or highly coloured. Stone objects could also be covered with it, or the sandy compositions which were moulded into a variety of shapes. Gradually the early glass-makers developed thicker and more stable glazes until an actual glass vessel was practicable. Probably the first instances of the use of glass were

[1]Jaroslav C. Vavra: *5,000 Years of Glass making*.

11

flat coloured sheets which were cut into various shapes for inlay or mosaic work.

The next phase in glass-making, which occurred about 1300 B.C., was important for it was discovered that heated glass could be gathered round a suitable cone of earth or clay and shaped with a flat knife whilst still in a plastic state. The cone was removed when the glaze was thick enough and a glass pot or jar was left.

Standing objects such as small vases or bottles could be made without fear of collapse; both translucent and transparent glazes were produced. Some surviving pieces show tiny hair cracks obviously caused by stresses and strains which appeared at some time or other during the experimental stages. A large number of attractive pieces, such as small ewers or jugs, with single or double handles, ointment holders and cosmetic containers, which were, according to ancient customs, buried with the owner, have been dug up. The mystery and beauty of glass is illustrated in these early objects some of which, through the action of the earth, have gained beautiful iridescent colours.

Decorative technique quickly improved and excellent workmanship was the mark of the Egyptian glass-makers who used glass for mosaic designs, figures of deities and sacred emblems as well as for containers and drinking vessels. Even coffins of glass were made and used, but the majority of pieces were vases, jugs, alabastrons (cigar-shaped containers with or without small looped handles), urns, amphorae (tall and pear-shaped, with very small bases) and oenochoae (jugs with curved handles and flat wider bases).

The art of glass-making spread rapidly to other countries bordering the Mediterranean. After its foundation in 331 B.C., Alexandria soon became the chief centre of the glass-making industry, obtaining control of the export trade and of the markets hitherto enjoyed by Egypt. It is likely that travelling glass-makers were responsible for introducing the craft to Rome, and after the conquest of Egypt in 27 B.C., glass began to reach this city in large quantities.

About 50 B.C. a dramatic step forward occurred when it was discovered that instead of using a solid iron 'pontil' rod for the whole operation, a hollow rod (subsequently called a blowing iron) could be dipped into a furnace and a batch (mixture of ingredient chemicals) gathered on the end. The batch would adhere to the rod, and when taken out could be blown into a hollow bubble. Once the flowing bubble had formed, it could be gradually expanded by pressure of a glass-blower's breath, and twisted and turned to keep it moving to resist the force of gravity until blown larger, worked upon and eventually formed into the desired article of reflective beauty.

Coloured Glass

All the earliest records and studies of glass, and the oldest specimens which have survived, prove without doubt that the ancient Egyptians neither wanted nor liked clear glass nor even glass with a mere suspicion of tints or colouring. Little of any clear glass that was made has survived.

In the surroundings of the Nile Valley and the colourful scenes of the streets and the magnificence of Egyptian architecture, where stone was also brightly painted, coloured glass must have seemed desirable, especially in contrast with the earthen vessels made for use. The Egyptians were certainly fond of rich colours, imitating semi-precious stones in glass of rich blues, yellows and reds. Dark and light blues were also popular. Three of the earliest dateable glass vessels are goblets and are all of turquoise blue—bearing the cartouche of King Thotmes III (1501-1449 B.C.); they are preserved in the British Museum, London, the Metropolitan Museum, New York and the Aegyptische Staatssammlung, Munich.

Roman and Grecian fragments have been analysed, proving that the early craftsmen were familiar with the use of several metals for tinting glass. These metals were copper, manganese and iron; azure blue, the predominant colour in ancient glass, being produced by the use of iron in different proportions with other metals. The Alexandrians developed their use of coloured glass at a very early period; dark azure blue was probably produced in their furnaces. Throughout the story of glass development, whether in Egypt, Alexandria, Rome, Syria, the near East, Europe, or Venice, the accent was on producing colour in glass vessels, and a higher degree of technological skill was required from the earliest times to meet this demand. It seemed natural that coloured glass took first place amongst the accomplishments of the early glass-makers since the techniques at their disposal, before the use of the blowing iron was discovered, demanded great individuality. Patterns and designs were the very centre of their work and this led them to experiment endlessly with different methods, probably the most common of which was to overlay strips of different coloured glass of varying widths on the body of the vessel, giving a combed effect, sometimes waved and sometimes zigzagged.

Advances in glass-making in no way superseded the continued use of coloured glass and it remained as popular as ever. Some pieces were shaded by adding oxides and others were decorated by gilding or enamelling, these two being made permanent and protected from wear by firing.

While the Egyptians made their glass within the boundaries of their own well protected country, the Romans proved more eclectic and drew techniques and styles from every nation with whom their armies and civilization came in contact. This was especially so after Egypt fell to Augustus. Then followed the most important advance in the craft—the art of glass-blowing, which naturally extended enormously the variety of design, types and uses of the articles produced.

Throughout the Roman period, however, the accent remained on coloured glass, and even the great mass of popular vessels associated with the Seine-Rhine area are of pale green—a colour which was to remain dominant in the vernacular tradition in Britain for a thousand years. The finest products of Roman glass-making, of which the cameo-cut Portland vase is the epitome, were not to be equalled in the North of Europe until the 18th century; but throughout the middle ages the early traditions lived on in Venice.

After Syria came under Egyptian dominion in 1468 B.C., glass-making developed in that country and thereafter spread to many other countries, including a wide area under Islamic rule. From here it was carried to Venice. The long tradition of the Venetian glass-makers is no part of this book, except in so far as Venetian styles moulded British manufacture in the 17th century and influenced it again in the 19th; but it is important to realise that in every advance of glass-making, and in every shift of area, the glass produced was coloured, whether it was the thinly blown forms of the Syrian pieces, which were mostly pale blue-green, or the green tint of those of Alexandrian provenance, where artistic techniques reached an extremely high standard and a high percentage of luxury glass was made, or Venice itself.

Colour was used not only in the glass itself in ancient times and in mediaeval Venice, but also in its decoration. Mention has already been made of painting and gilding on Egyptian pieces: much Roman glassware was decorated in this manner and so were Syrian and Islamic pieces. In later times, Venetian craftsmen produced beautiful designs in enamel, and in Bohemia and Germany a tradition developed of painting on glass which covered a variety of scenes, figures, mottoes and elaborate coats of arms.

In the context of this long history of decorated glass, the English supremacy of the 18th century in plain glass seems remarkable. After the discovery by George Ravenscroft of the use of oxide of lead to make glass stable and durable for everyday use, clear lead glass triumphed in Britain for more than two hundred years. Even so, time was found in glass-houses to add colour to the wares which were made, or to make them of coloured glass. Three classic examples survive from the period immediately after that of Venetian imports—an attractive purple squat-shaped bottle decorated with trellis moulding in the Victoria and Albert Museum, South Kensington, another almost identical in the Marshall collection in the Ashmolean Museum, Oxford, and the beautiful sapphire blue double-handled base in the Toledo Museum in America. Thereafter, there were distinct uses of colour in England and Ireland right through to the 19th century. Although, as far as is known, no coloured heavy baluster stem glasses of the period 1690-1720—that of the finest of British drinking vessels—have been recorded, those of the subsequent 18th century stem groups in green and very occasionally blue come on the market at regular intervals.

Green glass, in most forms of vessels, was manufactured until the 19th century and the vogue for colour spread out into table glass of all types, culminating in the great period of the West of England factories, the Midlands and the North, and in Ireland. Milk and cream jugs, sugar basins, bowls and decanters were predominant in this period and the colours chiefly used were amethyst, red, green, blue, and white opal. Some of the colouring chemicals generally used in glass-making are described in a later chapter.

Then, also in the 18th century, clear glass in Britain was decorated in fashions looking back to more ancient traditions—the use of coloured canes in the stems of wine glasses, the elaborate painting and gilding done at Newcastle, Bristol, Yarmouth and other factories, and the reintroduction of the cameo by Tassie and Apsley Pellatt. By the end of the 19th century, coloured glass for the handmade market was far more fashionable than clear glass, and when the latter was used, it tended to have additions in colour. A whole range of new techniques was added to the repertoire: the addition of new chemicals, the invention of new types of glass, the introduction of overlay—in which a vessel of one colour was encased in glass of another—and the use of mould-blowing and press-moulding. Throughout the 19th century, decoration by painting, gilding, transfer printing and etching was continued.

Collectors of English glass tend to specialise in the clear glass which characterised the most accomplished period, but even then it is hard not to diversify into the acquisition of coloured glass. Almost as complete a collection could, for example, be made of the stem groups of green glasses as of clear ones in the later 18th century. No collector of 19th century glass can possibly ignore coloured specimens. To say that the age of 'glass of lead' is a momentary aberration in the long history of glass-making would not, however, be true—and after the 19th century, the British industry reverted, apparently irrevocably, to clear glass production. But British coloured glass has a right to be considered as a subject in itself; one, moreover, which has a greater number of connections with the earlier history of glass-making and many of whose techniques are revived from antiquity. The subject has rarely been studied in its own right and, in the past, American collectors have concentrated more on this field than their British counterparts. There are many similarities in the work of American and British factories in the 19th century, which may partly account for this, a trend which can easily be assessed in American collections, especially that of the Corning Museum of Glass, New York. But an increasing interest in 19th century coloured glass may now be seen in the lively market for these articles which continues to grow in salerooms on both sides of the Atlantic.

1. Origins of British Glass

Roman glass is a general term applied to pieces made during the period of the Roman Empire; because of the long duration of this period and the flourishing trade in glass-ware, it is by no means easy to establish the origin or exact date of specific pieces. Glass-making in Britain began with the Roman occupation, but the excavation of glasses alone does not establish that they were made here. The remains of likely Roman glass-houses have been found in various parts of the country and it has been common to find specimens, all of the well known pale green shade. Fragments of window glass, small bottles and specimens, mostly bowls showing the raised rib decoration, have been excavated. On the whole the evidence does not suggest a very high degree of glass-making art in Britain; the finest pieces were imported from abroad, at least until the 4th and 5th centuries A.D.

To the pale green of Roman glass has now been added the effect of nature: the marvellous film of iridescence caused by centuries beneath the earth which adds, to the most ordinary bowl or beaker, decoration beyond the art of man.

Britain did not entirely lag behind the Continent; and many unusual techniques were adopted, not least among them being the development of the Egyptian invention of producing vessels by the mosaic method. Fragments of coloured glass were arranged side by side and fused together in a pattern to make a complete vessel. Also copied were the famous 'Murrhine' bowls, of greater antiquity, about whose origin Pliny and other authors had speculated. They may have been made from natural stone, possibly a sort of jade, and glass bowls or other pieces were made in imitation, showing mixed streaky colours. Coloured canes and applied trails of opaque white glass began to be used quite frequently, especially on the bases of bowls and rounded jugs. Trailing round the necks of bottles appeared at a later period, possibly in the 8th or 9th centuries, and some examples have been excavated in England, although these were probably part of the stock of a travelling salesman from the Continent.

At this time, in the so-called Dark Ages, when in fact the trade routes with Europe were still open and when at least in the South and West of England relatively civilized society survived, a great quantity of glass was imported from the glass-houses of the Seine and Rhine districts, or was brought over by travellers. Green, once more, was the predominant colour and the glass took the form of beakers, jugs, bottles and bowls; but there were also bottles decorated with opaque blue and white trailed ornament and goblets with white and gold trailing.

The import of glass to England never died out and by the early Middle Ages took the form of *waldglas*. Waldglas in Germany and Northern Europe meant forest glass, because the glass-makers working inland used potash obtained from burning bracken or beech wood. It was known as *verre de fougère* in France and was popular in mediaeval times, especially in the well wooded areas of the Rhine. The colours were yellow, amber and green; a wide series of vessels was made with applied lumps of molten metal in various shapes, the most typical being known as prunts. These had become fashionable all over Northern Europe by the 15th century. Waldglas was rarely clear in texture and although it formed what has been called a 'degenerate' phase of the art of glass-making, this common glass has continued to be made almost to the present day. It grew out of the tradition of ordinary green Roman glass and both in style and content it proved to be the origin of glass-making in Britain.

Very little can be stated about specifically English manufacture in the early mediaeval period but in the context of the wealth of certain sections of the English economy, particularly the export of wool, it would be surprising if all glass had been imported from abroad. Apart from greenish window-glass, vernacular waldglas beakers, bowls and bottles may have been made in Kent before the 13th century, but no records or dateable specimens have been recorded.

At that time, probably to satisfy a demand arising out of the growing

Right
Dark green funerary urn from Avisford Romano-British burial cist. *c.* A.D. 350. 18 inches.

Worthing Museum Collection

wealth of the country, glass workers from Normandy came to the Weald of Kent and the well wooded areas of Sussex and Surrey, where they made clear and stained glass. Lawrence Vitrearius and his family were among others who settled in Chiddingfold in the 13th and 14th centuries and there is evidence that they used pale greenish metal characteristic of waldglas to make beakers, other drinking vessels, lamps and bottles, bowls, cups and other receptacles. Some were of blown glass and others moulded. One of their wares was the type of bottle in which doctors inspected their patients' urine—this use being recorded in a number of mediaeval illustrations.

Certain differences were appearing before the end of the Middle Ages which suggest that a characteristic English style was emerging, but it was only in the 16th century that the importance of glass-making in England really materialised. Emigrants from Lorraine settled among the earlier Norman families in the Weald and, first being chiefly window-glass makers, they slowly turned to the more difficult but more profitable manufacture of glass for household use.

Dark brown sealed bottles, *this page and opposite right* 17th century, *opposite left* early 18th.

Worthing Museum Collection

There was a period of Venetian imports after 1500 to meet a new demand for luxury glasses, decorated as no English maker yet could. Of the century before, the well-known Fairfax cup, a Venetian beaker decorated in enamels with a hunting scene, is a good example. Such things were rare and preserved perhaps in their own leather cases for use by the head of the family alone. But by the mid 16th century the use of glass for drinking had spread far beyond the small circle of the rich aristocracy. Even in merchant and yeoman households a new piece of furniture was to be found—a small, very narrow cupboard with an open front, enclosed by two doors with turned rails instead of panels. This hung on the wall and was almost certainly made to contain the half-dozen or so glasses of the house.

In the rapidly growing wealth of Elizabethan England it was not surprising that entrepreneurs seized on this new and expanding market. Jean Carré of Arras and Antwerp proposed to start in London 'crystal glass vessel making in the fashionable Venetian style'. Under his direction in 1570 the famous glass works were set up at the Crutched Friars, Aldgate,

Next page

Pale green Roman glass: two cone beakers, one decorated with opaque white trailing, the other with bands of glass thread (Seine-Rhine *c.* A.D. 450); and a fine goblet, wheel engraved with a hound chasing two hares and a Greek inscription: 'Use me and may you be happy'. Probably Alexandrian, A.D.400. All imported into England.

Worthing Museum Collection

London, and in 1575 a Venetian, Jacob Verzelini, probably one of Carré's men, obtained from Queen Elizabeth 'the sole right and privilege of making glass in London in the Venetian style.' A recent historian has described the impact of the new manufacture in vivid terms which contrast with the formal details of dates and factories.

'The upsurge of national energy was expressed in an increasing appetite for the elaborate and brilliant, and in the rapid development of prosperity which peace had made possible, there was a demand for glass. This fragile, glittering substance had precious estimation approaching that of jewels. Its transparency and colour were exciting to people who had seen little of it and before its present vulgarisation the idea of glass possessed an aesthetic value like that of the sea of glass in the Revelation of St. John. In 1575 the Venetian glass worker, Verzelini, was given a monopoly of glass-making provided he taught his craft to the Queen's "natural subjects" and fifteen glass-houses were set up under his supervision near his own in Crutched Friars. The sparkle of the wares affronted the eye of both the economist and the moralist; it betokened worldly extravagance and a misdirection of the national resources. *A Brief Examination of certain Ordinary Complaints* says;

"These eleven years there were not one of the haberdashers, not a dozen in all London, and now from the Tower to Westminster all along every street, full is of them and there shops glitter and shine of glass as well drinking as well looking-glass, yea all manner of vessel of the same stuff." The exciting use of glass in the open air was explored in great gardens. Bacon wanted a bathing pool with sides and bottom "embellished with COLOURED glass and

Mid-18th century drinking glasses.
Left to right
Mead glass with gadrooned bowl, waisted stem and domed foot. Wine glass with swelling knopped stem. Wine glass with shoulder stopped stem.

Seddon Collection

such things of lustre" but the fashionable enlargements of windows in the facades of great houses which caused the saying: "Hardwick Hall, more glass than wall" seemed to him at the end of the century to have been overdone. He said: "You shall have sometimes fair houses so full of glass that one cannot tell where to become to be out of the sun or cold." But to eyes as yet unaccustomed to its use, glass gave us a sense of magical luxury, of great riches in hand, of a brave new world.'[1]

Two more instances of the new fashion may be given: John Nicols in his *Progress of Queen Elizabeth* recorded that in 1578 when the Queen visited Hawstead Hall in Suffolk, this was a timber and plaster house; the plaster was thickly stuck with pieces of glass 'which made a brilliant appearance when the sun shone and even by moonlight.' And a broadside (date *circa* 1570–80) printed by J. D. Furnivall in his edition of Stubbs *Anatomy of Abuses* complains that in return for valuable exports of leather, tallow, beef, bacon and bell metal, 'into England there must bring bugles to make baubles, coloured bones, glass beads to make bracelets with all, for every day gentle women of England do ask.'

Up to this date those who were able to buy glass had been content with the green colour for generations. But the Venetian glasses, once the prerogative of the rich, inspired desire for the clear metal. This new demand explains Verzelini's triumphal career because his twenty-one year royal licence had included a monopoly and a prohibition on the importation of glass from overseas, shielding him from outside competition and allowing a period during which the knowledge of expert glass-making could be developed. Verzelini himself was seventy years old when he

[1]Elizabeth Jenkins—*Elizabeth the Great.* (Victor Gollancz, 1958), pp.162-3.

Mid-18th century drinking glasses.
Left to right
Wine glass with unusual blue-green metal, rare knopped stem and high domed foot. Rare wine glass with rounded bowl, knopped and opaque spiral stem and high domed foot. *c.* 1760. Wine glass with rare knopped stem and high domed foot.

retired and moved to Downe in Kent, a rich and respected man. He died in 1606 at the age of 84 and was buried in the parish church, where a brass tablet was set up in memory of his whole family. There are eight known surviving goblets which are attributed to him, most being decorated in diamond point engraving by the contemporary engraver of glass and pewter, Anthony de Lisle, one of the few engravers known to have been working between 1580 and 1602. The earliest dated glass is 1577. The stem and foot are missing, having been replaced by a 17th century pearwood foot and it has a narrow silver rim chased with egg and tongue motifs.

Apart from these very few examples, the late 16th and early 17th centuries are poorly represented by glasses made in England, although this may simply reflect the great rate of breakage; for the common green glass had now reached a price at which replacement was a problem rather than a tragedy. Experiments in the metal were continued by several makers, such as Sir Gerald Bowes, a soldier who took over Verzelini's business after his retirement in 1592. He was followed by others in fairly quick succession, but the industry did not prosper from such frequent changes of ownership. Indeed the whole of glass manufacture seems to have been overtaken by a depression, probably not unconnected with the continuing commercial crisis of the early 17th century.

In 1615 Sir Robert Mansell, a retired admiral with a distinguished career and a sound business head, entered the industry. Within a few years he gained complete control and in 1618 secured a monopoly from James I. He established new works or absorbed existing ones in all parts of the country and his monopoly lasted until his death in 1656, when,

18th century drinking glasses.
Left to right
Rare wine glass with ogee bowl and spiral stem, c. 1750. Wine glass with attractive rounded bowl and plain stem, c. 1730. Very rare wine glass with double ogee bowl and opaque spiral stem, c. 1755.

partly due to loss of enthusiasm and enterprise and partly to the unsettled state of the country, the industry again suffered a serious decline. Glass from the Mansell period is, even in museum collections, not well represented since no definite knowledge exists as to what constitutes the English style during those years.

Mansell's successor was the Duke of Buckingham (1628–87) whose keenness for making fine glass in the Venetian style led to a revival both of the import trade and of home manufacture. It may also have channelled the activities of the Glass-sellers Company which had received a Charter in 1635 and was engaged in promoting research for producing a better type of glass, because the existing soda glass was fragile and not durable. One of its members, active between 1667 and 1675, was John Greene who ordered glasses to be made to his own designs by Morelli of Murano and sent to England for sale. These designs, of which there are over four hundred, have been preserved and can be seen in the British Museum. The difficulties met with on this project, such as the fact that Greene found the glasses were not made to his liking and that a great number were lost by breakages in transit, led the Company, whose Charter was renewed in 1664, to concentrate still more on encouraging research at home. The chief trouble was the inferiority of the glass metal compared with the natural rock crystal—the standard by which the soda glass of the period was judged. Not even Roman glass had rivalled the natural material and for all the skill and patience of the Venetian workers, the metal, although pliable enough in the hands of the craftsmen to make artistic designs and shapes, lacked both weight and quality.

No invention in glass history is better known than that of George Ravenscroft, an English analytical chemist, who first added oxide of lead to his batches of ingredients. This tremendous step forward was the result of many years' experiments and produced a 'sort of crystalinne glass resembling rock crystal' as he called it. He was soon officially engaged by the Glass-sellers Company to conduct further experiments and was encouraged to carry on still more research to produce a clear crystal glass, which would combine the easy working properties of the Venetian cristalle with the strength necessary for table glass.

Ravenscroft set up his experimental glass works in the Savoy in 1673

Three drinking glasses showing stem and bowl variations. *c.* 1730 to 1780.
Seddon Collection

and employed Italian glass-makers as his assistants. He received a patent from the Glass-sellers Company and they installed him in a glass-works at Henley-on-Thames about two years later. His 'glass of lead' was the beginning of a truly English art and the heavy metal steadily superseded the thin soda glass of Venice; although for another half century the Venetian influence could be seen in the designs of some English drinking glasses, especially ale glasses.

To give confidence to his clients, Ravenscroft was given permission to attach a small glass seal, stamped with the head of a raven, on his better made pieces to show they were composed of his new metal. A small number of such specimens have survived: including the three in colour mentioned above. One of the main difficulties of these experimental years was glass sickness or crizzelling, through which the surface lost its brilliance and took on a crackled appearance. Ravenscroft was never fully successful in eliminating this and it was not until his successor, Hawley Bishopp, took over his work that the fault was completely overcome. Bishopp reopened the Savoy glass-house in 1682 and before long the rapid and widespread development of the English glass industry both created and supplied an increasing

Jug of vase shape with applied trailing.
c. 1770.

Seddon Collection

18th century milk or cream bowl with folded rim. Probably Nailsea, *c.* 1790.
Seddon Collection

demand for clear glass of lead, placing the English glass-houses in the fore-front of the European industry.

Green Glass Manufacture in The Vernacular Tradition

The use of decorative colour in the 18th century, following the period of these discoveries, is discussed in the next chapters, but the traditional manufacture of glass which had existed long before should not be forgotten. Local production of common glass for everyday use continued, still mainly green in colour. The greatest number of objects made were bottles, either for serving wine or storing it and of course for medicine and other liquids. The colour sometimes varied into blackish green or brownish 'bottle glass' and this long series of serving and wine bottles continued from the 16th century or earlier down to the 19th. Many of them bear dates, initials or names of owners, or such societies as University Common rooms, or designations in the form of applied seals; Samuel Pepys recorded in his diary that he ordered several dozen bottles of wine with his seal upon them. Such bottles form a collectable subject in themselves; and those not dated can be more or less divided into three main periods by their shapes.

1. The earliest form, 17th century, with a wide bulbous body, a short neck and a large 'kick' depression in the base; this continues to the first half of the 18th century.

2. Lengthened neck and body, wide shouldered and straight sides, convenient for stacking in cellars. These could also be brought up for serving at the table and lasted until about 1765.

Next page
Dark brown sealed bottles, 18th century.
Worthing Museum Collection

27

Cream jug of unusual colour. Bristol, c. 1780.

Seddon Collection

3. From about 1765 to the early part of the 19th century the bottles took on a more conventional appearance, which continued till the present day.

As the glass industry spread far beyond London in the 18th century, the production of common glass increased. Whereas only the better, more skilled glass-houses attempted the making of the fine baluster and later 18th century stem glasses and the contemporary decanters and other table ware, small and large houses as far apart as Devon, Northumberland and the Scottish Lowlands produced quantities of window glass and bottle glass. Apart from the bottles themselves, the green glass production followed, normally in cruder form, the styles of the clear lead glass; and a whole series of glasses, jugs, decanters, etc., can be found in shades from pale to dark green, and some in pale bluish green, from the 1720's for at least a century more. These articles are often attributed, quite wrongly, to Bristol; some, such as the early dark green mead glasses with gadrooned bowls and domed and folded feet, date from forty years before the Bristol factory started production. Probably the majority of the better specimens came from established areas, such as Stourbridge and Newcastle, but it is almost impossible to assign a location for them. They can however be dated, stylistically, as can all 18th century glass ware, although in the case of the cruder examples ten years should be added to allow for provincial resistance to changes of fashion. Some of the earlier examples still show the form and influence of the Venetian waldglas and wealden styles, but by the mid 18th century these had vanished and by 1800 green glass manufacture relates almost exactly to that of clear lead glass.

2. The Use of Decorative Colour

Following the period of Hawley Bishopp and the perfection of 'glass of lead', drinking glasses, goblets and table glass came from the glass-houses in and about London and Southwick in great profusion. For fifty years after 1690 London held its supremacy. Other fine glass-works grew up, notably in Newcastle, but in the period of the heavy baluster stem glasses it was London which produced the great mass of fine British glass.

The Excise Act of May 1695, passed by the Government to raise much needed money to finance the war against the French, authorised a duty of 20 per cent on flint glass and glass plate and one shilling a dozen on common glass bottles. There was such an outcry from all concerned in the industry that in 1698 it was halved and the next year discarded altogether. Its duration was not long enough nor the incidence heavy enough to discourage the manufacturers, but the Excise Act of 1745 was a different affair altogether. This Act laid a tax of nine shillings and fourpence per hundredweight on the materials used. It was once again caused by the need to raise funds for the professional wars then being waged on the Continent and it created a great burden for a full century. The immediate result was that the glass-maker had either to raise the price of his wares or use less glass in them by cutting down the size—a trend which had already begun with the evolution of the light baluster wine glasses. The majesty of the beautiful heavy baluster glasses, with their variety of stem formations, disappeared altogether from the market and even those with the lighter formation of knops gave way to the simple twists. Even the luxury of the folded foot (a double thickness of glass folded underneath to strengthen the rim) had to be discarded, although rare instances of this occur in all later glasses up to 1800.

The main effect of the duty was to divert much of the attention of the glass-makers from the intrinsic beauty of the glass itself, and the forms which could be created from it, to the decoration of the surface or the interior of the metal. Three main groups of wine glasses followed: those with plain stems, those with twists of air or opaque or coloured enamel, and those with facet cutting. Only in the middle group was colour used, but increasingly it came to be employed in the decoration of the surface by enamelling or gilding, and of course glasses of all these three stem periods can be found in green and occasionally greenish blue glass.

In the centre, a rare goblet with ogee bowl and coloured spiral stem. *c.* 1760.
Alexander Collection

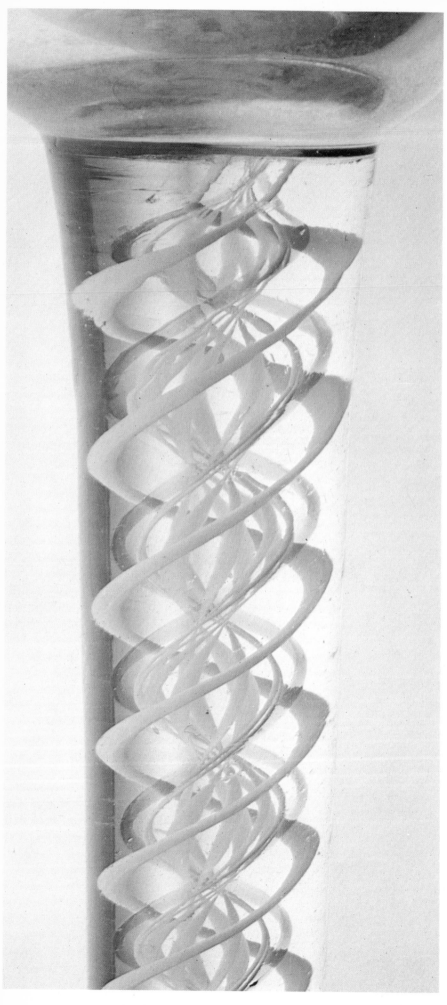

Detailed view of a fine triple series opaque and blue spiral stem. *c.* 1760.

Twisted Stems

The art of introducing white threads into glass was known and frequently employed by the Romans and more recently by the Venetians in *latticino* work. After the initial period of twisting air bubbles in the stem to make a spiral thread looking at first like mercury, came the introduction of white threads (or reintroduction, as the Verzelini goblet in the British Museum is encircled with two minute white enamel threads on the bowl). This development dates from about 1760 and was an intricate and complicated process. Lumps of white opaque glass were drawn out until almost wafer thin, then cut into lengths and introduced as more than one series or variety of twists or spirals in the stems, and entwined to make many different combinations: corkscrew, simple spiral, cotton, tape or multi-spiral. It is very common to find single or double series glasses but three or four series of distinct varieties in one pattern are now extremely rare. White stems were also introduced in candlesticks as well as champagne glasses and sweetmeats and occasionally in other English pieces. The same technique was of course used by the Italians and Germans and their work shows greater profusion, with threads even occurring in decanter stoppers.

The period of opaque twists brought a new and definite attraction to English glass, the effect of the bright decoration being to give a freshness not hitherto known. Those glasses with knops in the stems were few compared to the very large numbers of plain stemmed glasses which survived. Most of the glasses attributed to the Lynn factory in Norfolk come into this period. They have opaque twist stems and are all of very fine quality, showing the moulded horizontal ribbing on the bowl varying from two to seven lines characteristic of this factory.

Three wine glasses with rare opaque and coloured spiral stems. *c.* 1760.
Alexander Collection

Mixed Twist & Colour Twist Stems

Perhaps more decorative, and certainly more intricate, was the introduction of both air and opaque spirals in the same stem; these glasses are rare and are almost without exception found without knops. A small group, now widely sought after by collectors and rapidly increasing in price, contain spirals of coloured glass or enamel entwined with the opaque white threads. The rarest of the shades is canary yellow; other colours used were red, green, blue (the commonest) and a tartan mixture. Very occasionally, coloured spirals were used in conjunction with air twists.

Wine glass with opaque and blue spiral stem and engraved ogee bowl. *c.* 1760.
Alexander Collection

Above left
Group of rare wine glasses with coloured and opaque spiral stems, round funnel and moulded ogee bowls. *c.* 1765.
Alexander Collection

Below left
Pair of wine glasses with opaque white twist edged in green and white.
Wyatt Collection
Ale glass with pair of spiral opaque white and blue twists.
de Wesselow Collection

Next page
Wine glass with opaque white and canary-yellow thread. Another with similar threads and moulded bowl, and a mixed twist—single red thread and air spiral.
de Wesselow Collection

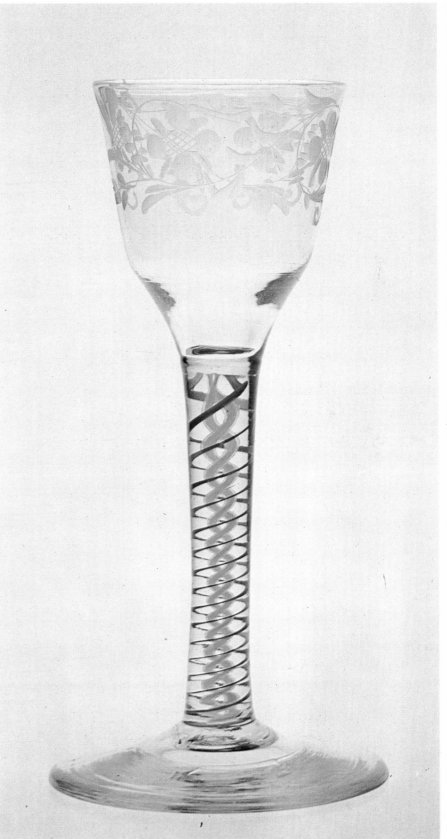

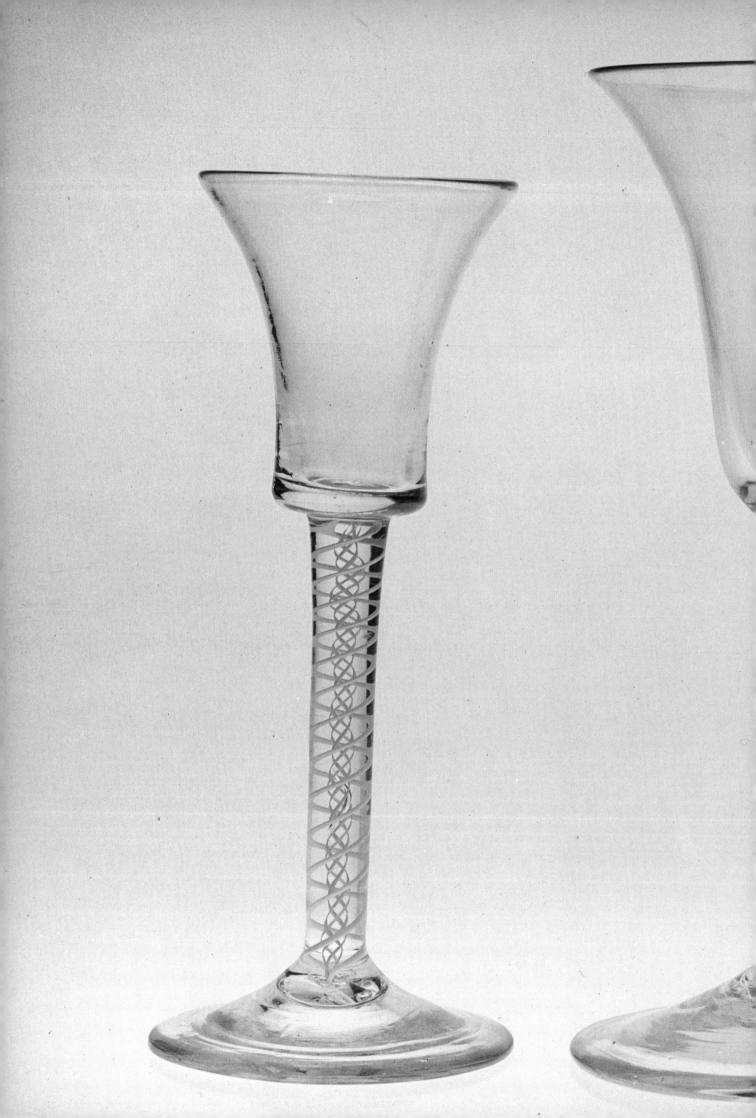

The great success of the glasses made with air and opaque twists encouraged the English craftsmen to experiment with these variations and probably a hundred or more existed. But the relative scarcity of colour twists suggest that fewer were made; a fact possibly explained by the tax which had been placed on enamel and also perhaps by the great difficulty of working with the material. In all 18th century examples the design of the bowls differed and no particular shape of bowls was associated with air, opaque, mixed or coloured stems.

Very rare wine glass with wheel engraved hunting scene and double series coloured spiral stem. *c.* 1765.

Alexander Collection

3. After 1750

As well as the opaque and colour twist stems, there were other uses of colour in the glass metal up to 1750, although these did not necessarily follow from the imposition of the Excise Tax. Glasses and table ware in colours of green, blue, opaque white and sometimes ruby red started to flow from the glass-houses. Decanters, jugs and bowls were also made, in sets like the glasses themselves, and surprisingly the most popular and sought after colour today is green.

Colour in glass proved to be as popular in 18th century England as it had been in other countries in earlier times, but at the same time its production involved many problems in furnace conditions. However, it is apparent from the vast quantity of coloured pieces which have survived that these were largely overcome; the depth of tone, especially in the blue and green of the Bristol decanters, jugs and scent bottles, leaves nothing to be desired.

The method of colouring glass at that time was straightforward and had indeed been practised since the late 17th century. Although the greatest

Interesting double wine glass with applied 'prunts'. *c.* 1760.

J. G. Littledale Collection

period for blue glass was 1780 to 1820, as far back as 1695 glass-makers were asking the Government of that day for relief from the heavy tax which had been imposed on glass, because among the materials imported into the country for glass making was smalt, a vitreous form of cobalt oxide.[1] Small quantities of the colouring agent required were simply added to the glass mixture itself. Some of the colour agents in current use in the mid 18th century were as follows:

[1]c.f. John Bedford: *British and other Coloured Glass* (Cassell & Co. Ltd., 1954) p.27.

Colour	Agent
Red	Gold, iron, copper.
Blue	Oxide of cobalt and copper.
Yellow	Silver, iron, antimony.
Green	Copper, iron, chromium.
Purple	Same as red and blue.
Orange	Carbon, sulphur.
Black	Zaffer, magnesia, copper, iron.

Opaque white or white opal glass could be produced if arsenic, calcium, tin, fluorspar, calcium phosphate and certain salts were added.

Interesting wine glass with opaque stem and foot. Late 18th century.
J. G. Littledale Collection

Pair of Bristol decanters of club shape.
Cecil Davis Limited

Coloured glass was probably made at all the main factories in Britain in the late 18th century and the 19th, but certain factories became more famous for their colour than any other glass; each of these was known for its own distinctive types and character of ware.

The well known phrase 'Bristol blue' was, and still is, applied to the majority of pieces of this colour. While this is not strictly accurate as a description of every piece of blue glass, Bristol was the home of most, if not all, of the best quality pieces. These were being made at the three 'flint, glass and

Bristol

ordinary' factories, as John Houghton noted as early as 1696, and indeed the Italian family of Dagnia were making country or common pieces of coloured glass from 1651. Manufacture extended to other glass-houses in the Bristol area as time went on and as trade increased both at home and overseas. The two most famous factories were at Redcliffe-back and in Temple Street. A royal visit to Bristol was described in the *Daily Post* of 14 November, 1738: 'Bristol, November 11th. Yesterday the Prince and Princess of Wales paid their promised visit to the city . . . the Companies of

Bristol decanters. *c.* 1790.
Cecil Davis Limited

42

the city made a most magnificent appearance in their formalities, marching two by two preceding the Corporation and the Royal guests. The Company of Glassmen went first, dressed in holland shirts on horseback, some with swords, other with crowns and sceptres in their hands made of glass.'

The best Bristol pieces which were most popular were beautifully rich blue quart and pint size decanters, some of tapering shape, others of more squat design, with and without neck rings. Fine gilding was used to decorate them and to indicate the contents by gilt simulated labels with chains and

Small flute cut decanter. *c.*1810.
Cecil Davis Limited

Next page
One of a pair of rare early Irish dishes, illustrating typical flat geometric cutting. *c.* 1780.

Cecil Davis Limited

Set of four very rare Irish salts decorated
with a moulded design. *c.* 1780.
Cecil Davis Limited

Flute cut tea caddy with Sheffield Plate
mount. *c.* 1780–1800.

Cecil Davis Limited

46

Wine glasses showing stem variations. Bristol, late 18th century.

Seddon Collection

Group of drinking glasses of the 18th century.

Middleton Collection

corresponding initials of the wine or spirit on the pear-shaped or bull's-eye stoppers. The labels were either six-sided, oval or rectangular, or less frequently in the shape of a shield. The usual number in a set of decanters was three or four, and metal stands covered with leather were supplied. Charming little sets of condiment bottles were also made for the table, in miniature, with similar designs in names and initials. Some of these decanters and other objects like bowls have the addition of shoulder and base flute cutting and some have no ornamentation at all. Some of the best

decanters were cut all over with facets, these being the earliest examples of English cutting; and diamond cutting in octagonal shapes, particularly on bottles, became common by the end of the 18th century. Sugar bowls were made bearing the letter 'S' on the cut finials, and also full cruet sets in wooden stands and sets of perfume bottles. Two of the very few decorators known for certain in this period are associated with Bristol: Isaac Jacobs and Michael Edkins—names which will be considered later on.

Other table glass in blue was made at Bristol, such as finger bowls, wine

Examples of thinly blown glass; probably Bristol, *c.* 1790.

Seddon Collection

48

glass coolers (bowls with two lips), cream jugs, sugar bowls and salt cellars. Sometimes the smaller productions were decorated with wrythen moulding.

Green was apparently also a popular colour, but much less of this deep rich shade has survived than the more prolific blue. Correspondingly, decanters, jugs and bowls are now rare. Surprisingly, however, all the sets of wine glasses of various designs with knopped and plain stems, some flute cut, others with plain bowls, are green; but there are no goblets; and no sets of blue glasses or water jugs were made there. The bottle trade flourished over a long period, the leading firm, Ricketts & Co., stamping their name on the bases of their products.

Little has been written about amethyst coloured glass. There is no reason why it should not have been made at Bristol. Very attractive pieces have survived, especially cream and milk jugs, bowls and vases, some plain, others with wrythen moulded decoration, as well as wine glasses and finger bowls. Genuine 18th century ruby glass is extremely rare and there can be no definite attribution to any pieces that come to light; but it is more than likely that the glass workers of this leading sea port of the West Country had the recipe for making it.

Stourbridge

Stourbridge has been described as one of the earliest centres of English glass-making and the only one to survive and grow steadily over the vicissitudes of some three and a half centuries. The factory was established by Lorraine glass-makers in the 16th century. The 1951 exhibition at the Festival of Britain illustrated how vast a contribution this district had made to the glass industry. But, until the 19th century, Stourbridge followed the current trends and fashions of the period and its productions are less distinctive than its continuous history would lead one to expect.

Bristol cream jug and sugar bowl with trellis moulded pattern. *c.* 1790.
Seddon Collection

Bristol cream jug and sugar bowl with rare moulded pattern. *c.* 1790.
Seddon Collection

Bristol 'bonnet' glass with trellis moulded pattern. *c.* 1790.
Seddon Collection

Cream jugs probably made at Bristol.
Late 18th century.

Seddon Collection

Bristol cream jug of design similar to the
glass opposite.

Seddon Collection

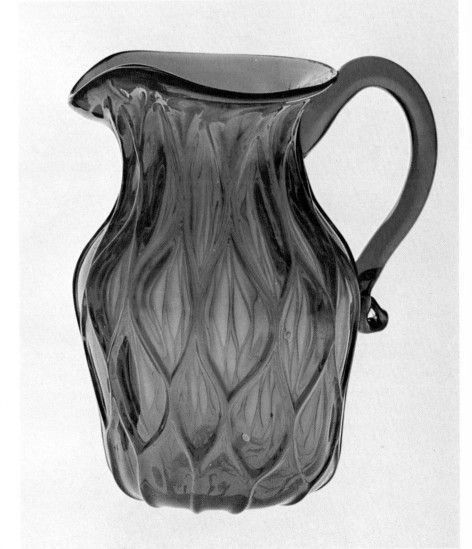

Next page
Group of chemists' jars and stoppers.
Early 19th century.

Seddon Collection

Group of 'egg cup' vases with folded rims showing colour variations. Late 18th century.

Seddon Collection

[1]Quoted in Geoffrey Wills: *The Country Life Pocket Book of Glass.*

Coloured glass formed a large part of the 18th century manufactures; 'in 1751 a traveller in the Midlands noticed that coloured glass was being made at Stourbridge "famous for its glass manufactures, especially for its coloured glass with which they make painted windows, which is here coloured in the liquid of all the capital colours in their several shades".'[1] There is little doubt, on the other hand, that public demand stimulated similar production in many other places and it is likely that such wares were made also at London and Newcastle and elsewhere.

According to a list set down by F. Buckley, two of the eight glass-houses producing flint glass in 1760 were making enamel glass: Denhams and the Audnam Flint. At one time it was the general theory that most 18th and early 19th century coloured glass came from the West·of England, from Bristol and Nailsea in particular, but it has been established for many years that articles in cobalt blue were made at other centres, in London, Stourbridge, Newcastle, Sunderland and Warrington, and no doubt their manufacture became fairly general throughout the country. Indeed the whole conception of Nailsea as an area manufacturing coloured and domestic glass-ware has recently been called in question, since the original records suggest that its main trade was in crown and window glass (see below).

A large quantity of small table pieces of rather coarser glass was made at the Stourbridge and also at the Birmingham factories, including small jugs and bowls of opaline texture, less dense than the opaque Bristol pieces. White opaque cream jugs and sugar bowls show a 'sunset glow' when held up to the light.

Ireland

[2]Quoted in Dudley Westropp: *Irish Glass.*

Cream jugs showing variations in colour and design. Bristol, late 18th century.

Typical Bristol cream jug and sugar bowl, the latter with high domed base. *c.* 1790.

Seddon Collection

It is perhaps less well known that many attractive items of coloured table glass were made in Ireland. One J. Wright from Waterford, in a letter of 1835 to his brother, stated 'We have three very nice half pint flasks made of beautiful blue glass.'[2] Isaac Warren, one of the firm's best customers in Dublin, when ordering glass in 1835, asked for green pickle pots and blue butter coolers, and in another letter from the glass-works, half pint flasks of a blue colour are mentioned.

Mr. Dudley Westropp owned a dark blue finger bowl marked underneath 'Penrose Waterford' and in the old Waterford account books are numerous

55

Small amethyst jug, probably Bristol c. 1790.

Worthing Museum Collection

entries of payments for green cullet. Cullet consisted of broken pieces of glass from items discarded during the making or bits which were broken off by workmen. It was all melted down again and used in fresh gatherings of metal. Sometimes quantities were sold to other glass works.

A very attractive series of Irish productions are blue and green jam or marmalade bowls and covers, as well as tea caddies which were made in the prolific 1780-90 period. They were usually fitted with silver rims. (See illustration on p. 46).

4. Painted Glass

Royal Beilby goblet illustrating the best of their coloured enamelling. *c.* 1760.
Alexander Collection

Enamel on Plain Glass

Clear glass goblets, wine glasses and plain fruit bowls were made in large quantities during the 18th century and even at the present time are not valuable in themselves; but those with enamel decoration and designs are a different matter. Enamelling in colours on glass was practised from ancient times and continued undiminished in many European countries more recently. Some of the best work was executed in Germany and Bohemia where artists usually selected involved coats of arms, crests and other heraldic devices, and painted them in brilliant colours. This work was at its peak in the 15th and 16th centuries but continued long afterwards and was reproduced in the 19th century. Both coloured and clear glasses were enamelled in Venice, and artists were also skilful in gilding.

Two main types of painting on glass were in use, one permanent and one in which the design was only painted on and gradually wore off according to the amount of handling to which the particular article was subjected. In some instances paintings of the latter type were treated with varnish to render them more permanent. The description of the permanent process was set out clearly by the late E. M. Elville: 'the enamel is made up in the

Fine goblet with armorial design by the Beilby family. Double series opaque twist stem. *c.* 1760.

Corning Museum of Glass

form of a paste consisting of a substance intended to assist fusion, known as a flux, a finely powdered metallic colouring compound, and an oil or water medium which is added to give the paste the necessary consistency. The paste is applied by a brush, transfer or other means, after which the article is fired in a muffle or kiln until the flux has melted, dissolved the colouring medium and assumed a uniform glazed finish with the glass body.'[1]

In 1689 a most enlightening book was published. Written originally in French by H. Blancourt, it was translated into English and shows the deep interest that was shown in the decoration of glass. The title page reads—

Part of the preface refers to the decoration of glass: 'Glass may receive, either within or without, any sort of metallic colours which make it very proper for painting. Those which we shall teach to extract from metals show in this book for the tinging of glass, give it a lustre equal to precious stones and set it off with unspeakable beauty . . . and besides what relates to the art of making glass, we also treat of the ways of painting on enamel and glass; and we do also show the way of extracting tinctures of several colours, of herbs, flowers, roots, grain; wood, stones and other things for this sort of painting and tinging of glass. Although this art of painting seems different from that of glass, yet they ought not to be separated since this painting is performed with minerals and that they melt in fire like that of the enamel.'

Probably the earliest painter on glass in England inserted an advertisement in the *Postman*, 3rd December, 1696, 'Mr. Gullet, enameller, makes and sells all sorts of works enamelled and of glass, different postures of all kinds, animals, plants, trees, flowers and fruit together with all manner of representations to the life. In short, whatever can be desired or thought on either in glass or enamelled in the fire. Without using anything besides his hand or the matter. He lives at the sign of the Castle, St. Martins lane.'[2]

No specimens of this artist's work, as far as is known, now exist nor have any from such an early period survived, but of those mentioned above, one of the Verzelini goblets bears traces of gilding. Decoration by enamel painting was rarely practised in this country at any time, but the

[1]E. M. Elville: *The Collector's Dictionary of Glass*, page 78.

THE ART OF GLASS
shewing
How to Make all Sorts of Glass,
Crystal and Enamel. Likewise
the Making of Pearls, Precious Stones,
China and Looking Glasses.
To Which is Added
the Method of Painting on Glass
and Enamelling. Also how to
Extract the Colours from Minerals,
Metals, Herbs and Flowers.
A Work Containing Many Secrets
and Curiosities Never Before Discovered.
With an Appendix Containing
Instructions for Making Glass Eyes
Of All Colours.

[2] Quoted in Francis Buckley, *Old English Glasses.*

The Beilby Family

name of Beilby has become a by-word to collectors of specimen glasses and fortunately enough of those decorated by members of this talented family have survived to indicate the style of their work and the types of scenes and motifs which they applied.

The history of the family is well documented. William Beilby, the senior member (1706–65) was born at Scarborough and later moved to Durham where he set up a good business as a jeweller and silversmith. He married in 1733 and brought up a family of seven children, five sons and two daughters. Apparently all had artistic leanings but only William and Mary are recorded as painters on glass. By 1760 the family had moved to Newcastle-on-Tyne, where Ralph Beilby (1743–1817), a wood engraver, took on an apprentice, Thomas Bewick, and in 1777 the latter was taken into partnership with Ralph. Later, Bewick wrote his autobiography called 'A Memoir of Thomas Bewick. Written by himself', and he recorded the details of the Beilby family. When he joined the Beilby household about 1767, both William and Mary Beilby (who would then be aged 27 and 18 respectively) 'had constant employment of enamel painting on glass.' William had learnt the art of enamelling in Birmingham, where he had worked for a time as an enamel box maker. During his apprenticeship Berwick became attracted to Mary, but in her early twenties she had a paralytic stroke which appears to have made her an invalid and ended any thought of marriage or further work.

The first enamelled work on glasses appeared about 1762, the decoration being of an heraldic nature in coloured and white enamels and there can be no doubt that such glasses were decorated by William, as Mary at that

Wine glass, the round funnel bowl painted with a rare pastoral scene by the Beilbys of Newcastle. Double series opaque stem. *c.* 1760.

Alexander Collection

Next page
Enamelled glasses: wine glass with vine pattern in white and green.
de Wesselow Collection
Glass with fruiting vine pattern.
Wine glass with simple floral pattern.
Wyatt Collection

time would have been only thirteen. It is known that Ralph Beilby was an heraldic engraver and probably influenced his elder brother William in the type of decoration which he painted. About 1774, however, the style changed and the scope was widened to include naturalistic motifs, rustic subjects, landscapes and conventional and fanciful scenes. Probably Mary Beilby assisted in the enamel painting of these glasses but it is not possible to distinguish their work as in nearly all cases where there is a signature, it is simply 'Beilby'. One goblet, however, has come to light bearing the signature 'W. Beilby'. The brother and sister left Newcastle-on-Tyne after the death of their mother in 1778, when they settled in Fifeshire and apparently discontinued their work.

Ralph, the expert in heraldry who was often employed to paint coats of arms on doors of coaches, was obviously a great help in advising William with his most important bucket bowl goblets on which he painted the Royal coat of arms of George III. Ralph also had a deep knowledge of birds and this influence can be seen in many of the rustic and landscape scenes. Almost without exception, the glasses, as would be expected from that period, have opaque twist stems and the great majority also have traces of gilt around the bowl rims.

As well as the Royal coat of arms, probably commemorating the birth of George III's eldest son, the Beilbys executed a number of armorial designs, mostly for Northumbrian or other Northern families and some of these are on as magnificent a scale as the Royal goblets. More typical of their general work, and obviously of wide popular appeal, were the country scenes, miniature pastoral landscapes often with figures, some in colour, the greater number in plain white. No precise categories can be given, for the number is considerable, but a distinction can be made between heavy brush work in white enamel and wash enamel, the latter being much rarer. The scenes can be divided into five main groups:

1. Sporting scenes, skating, hunting, shooting and fishing, all cleverly and most delicately painted in unmistakable style.
2. Landscapes with garden scenes and exotic and other birds.
3. Classical buildings and ruins with architectural features, including columns and obelisks.
4. Ale glasses with typical tall, round funnel bowls decorated with hops and barley motifs. Also decanters painted with white enamel labels similar to the engraved labels of the same period.
5. Simple designs, around the top of the bowls, of floral festoons or swags and vine motifs.

Other subjects are known, such as masonic emblems; and glasses other than drinking vessels were painted by the Beilbys. Some decanters of mallet shape bear coats of arms in colours as well as wine labels in white. Three dated examples which exist are all in the Victoria and Albert Museum: a flask decorated with a sportsman, a small tankard and a circular punch bowl.

English glasses painted in white and, very rarely, coloured enamel, by unknown artists come to light occasionally, but do not show the wealth of detail of the Beilbys and the colours are thin and poor. Subjects which are known are a portrait of Prince Charles Edward and a crest of an animal's head and various types and patterns of initials; also the very simple repetitive floral or vine motifs.

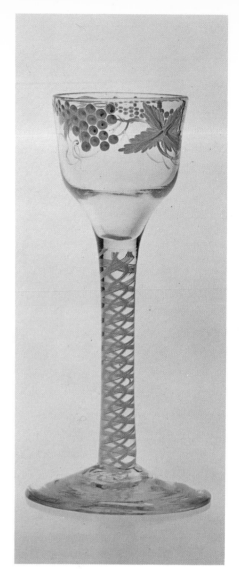

Edkins & Other Painters on Opaque Glass

Coloured glass was not the only form to be associated with Bristol in the late 18th century; white opaque glass, simulating porcelain, was equally well known. The body of the material was most suitable for decoration and a whole genre of painting, more akin to that practised on contemporary porcelain than on glass, grew up in and around Bristol, culminating in the very fine artistry of Michael Edkins.

The white opaque pieces were concentrated in the production of types more reminiscent of porcelain than of glass: candlesticks, vases, bowls, tea caddies (usually bearing the names of varieties of tea—'Green' and

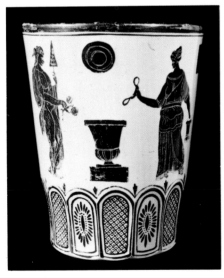

'Bohea') and condiment and scent bottles. All these things have become extremely rare and expensive and are now greatly prized by collectors. The tea caddies and sometimes candlesticks or tapersticks (small editions of the former to be placed on the slides of writing tables or secretaire bookcases) usually had loose Battersea enamel savealls to catch the melted wax. The great majority of the painted subjects were brilliant bouquets of flowers and exotic birds; less frequently, Chinese figure scenes and landscapes are found.

Michael Edkins (1734–1811) was born in Birmingham and moved to Bristol when he was 20. He married the daughter of a Bristol glass-maker and was made a Burgess of the City. The ledger account which he kept of his work is preserved in the City Art Gallery. He painted glass, and Bristol delft ware, as well as travelling coaches, and he decorated scenery and property for the stage. A man of many talents, he was also a fine musician. Edkins certainly executed some of the finest work in enamel on opaque white Bristol glass; although, as with all cases where only the name of one artist working on a whole range of items is known, much more is attributed to him than the evidence justifies.

There were undoubtedly other artists working in the same style during this period; all that can be inferred is that their technique was inferior and their colours dull in appearance.[1] Falling in the category of workshop productions, and of lesser importance, were mugs, basins, cream jugs and small vases in the opaque white glass decorated with designs of lesser detail and often in cruder brush work. Probably other areas copied the style of enamel painting, although, as mentioned above, the Midland opaque glass is of a different, more translucent quality than that of Bristol.

63

Gilding

As a method of decoration, gilding on glass was one of the first in the ancient and classical periods, and in Venice and Bohemia it was used consistently, either with or without other forms of painting. A great deal of Continental glass in the 18th century was gilded, in Holland and France, as well as Germany, and in Spain at the Royal factory of San Ildefonso de la Granja. Many of these pieces are made in coloured glass and a series of dark green and dark red wineglasses and goblets is not easy to distinguish from Bristol. Sets of small dark red glasses were also made, usually with similar glass trays to match. The main distinction is that the continental glasses are more elaborately and heavily cut; and also that few English *coloured* wineglasses were actually gilded, this form of decoration being restricted mainly to coloured decanters, bowls, etc.

Some gilt labels are found on clear glass decanters, but these are much less common than the blue and green ones, just as on clear pieces like fingerbowls and wine coolers gilding is extremely rare. By contrast, gilding occurs in a number of cases on clear wine and ale glasses and larger goblets of the opaque twist period, in the form of floral sprays and bouquets, twisting vines or hops, according to the liquid they were intended to hold. The painting is usually fine and expert and, if it has not worn, the gilding contrasts magnificently with the bright opaque white twists of the stems. Some of these glasses were also gilded on the foot, repeating the pattern, with a plain gilt rim. Similarity in the style of painting and the fact that almost all these glasses are from the same stem period, suggest that they came from one particular factory. There is no reason to assign them to Bristol, but they may well be attributed to a

A rare goblet and a champagne glass decorated with vine sprays in fired gilt on double series opaque twist stems. *c.* 1760.
Alexander Collection

Right
Decanter *c.* 1765 painted by the Beilby family with Port label and surrounding decoration of vines and a butterfly in white enamel. 12 inches.

Wyatt Collection

London glass-house employing a skilled artist or artists, possibly immigrants from Europe.

There were two kinds of gilding employed in England at this date: straightforward painting, which tended to wear off quickly, and which was confined to less elaborate and cheaper pieces; and a way of applying the design during the making of the article, while it was still in a plastic state. The article was then fired, usually without a flux. Another attractive process, though one used mainly on the Continent, and termed 'eglomisé', consisted of working the subject in gilt on the back of the surface to be seen, and protecting it with varnish and metal foil on a second layer of glass.

In the art of gilding coloured glass, Bristol produced another maker whose documentary history has survived, chiefly because his name appears in gilt as a signature on blue decanters, wine glass coolers (sometimes decorated with the Greek key pattern and sometimes with a reindeer crest) and on stands or plates. This was Isaac Jacobs, who worked with Lazarus Jacobs, his father, at their glass-house in Temple Street, Bristol—where Isaac was duly appointed 'Glass Manufacturer to His Majesty' (George III).

In 1806 Lazarus Jacobs advertised that he had 'specimens of the Dessert Set, which I. Jacobs had the honour of sending to Her Majesty, in burnished gold upon Royal purple coloured glass, to be seen at his Manufactory, where several Dessert Sets of the same kind are now completed from Fifteen Guineas per set to any amount.'[1]

Both father and son are mentioned in the Bristol Directory as being in business from 1775 till 1800 and the firm appears to have been very profitably established. According to the ledger of Michael Edkins, they employed him between the years 1785 and 1787 to decorate their blue glass in gilt work, and it has recently been suggested[2] that the gilt labelling on decanters signed 'I. Jacobs, Bristol' may, in fact, be identified as the work of Edkins. Edkins' ledger contains the entry '2 gold Decanters and Glasses decorated for Lazarus Jacobs', and 'To 6 five galln. jars Blue a Gold Scroll and Wrote'. Here is, drawn in the margin of the ledger, a simple scrolled label enclosing the word 'RUM'. The Bristol Gazette, of

Right

Typical examples of Bristol green decanters with gilt labels and initialed stoppers. *c.* 1790.

[1]Quoted by Geoffrey Wills: *The Country Life Pocket Book of Glass*, pages 204-205.

[2]R. J. Charleston, who has carried out an exhaustive research on the career of Michael Edkins. c.f. *Journal of the Society of Glass Technology*, Vol. XXXVIII, 1954, pages 10-11.

Two pairs of miniature dark green decanters for sauces, with gilt labels, 4 inches. Bristol: the pair with pinnacle stoppers *c.* 1770, the others *c.* 1790.

Hutchinson Collection

21st April, 1796, carries the notice 'Died in the Great Garden, Mr. Lazarus Jacobs a Jew and eminent glass merchant.'

Probably the finest examples of gilt decoration can be seen on a decanter and perfume bottle in the Victoria and Albert Museum and on a pair of decanters, recently sold at Christies for 4,000 guineas; after the style of James Giles, they portray exotic birds with floral designs and are of mallet shape with pinnacle stoppers, *circa* 1760.

Two more names have been recorded as painters or enamellers on glass.

William Absolam, an independent enameller of Great Yarmouth was in business as a glass-maker in the latter part of the 18th and early 19th century. He painted clear and opaque white and blue glass, mostly cream jugs, in both gilt and enamel. His favourite inscription was 'A Trifle from Yarmouth' accompanied by initials; and his gilt work on blue goblets with square bases and barrel shaped ornaments also in blue glass, are to be identified by occasional specimens which came to light bearing his initials.

James Donovan worked with his son in Dublin between 1770 and 1829. They owned a glass-house and also decorated china and pottery, some specimens of which were apparently signed 'Donovan, Irish Manufacture'. None of these have been discovered, but Dudley Westropp states in his book on Irish Glass that the contemporary records mention the existence of this enamelled glass; and there are accounts of orders, and correspondence about it between one factory and another. Perhaps some specimens may yet come to light.

Previous page
Fine examples of gilding: two ale glasses and a wine glass. *c.* 1760 and *c.* 1730.
Alexander Collection

Octagonal Bristol decanters with typical labels in fired gilt. *c.* 1800.
Cecil Davis Limited

Right
Pair of decanters and two bottles with unusual moulding. North Country origin, first quarter of the 19th century.
Seddon Collection

5. The Early 19th Century

New Uses of Coloured Glass

No clear line divides the coloured glass manufacture of the 18th from that of the 19th century. Bristol continued to make blue or green glass unchecked, save by the lack of imported cobalt during the Napoleonic war—as a result of which the colour changed temporarily to a paler ultramarine. The Midland factories grew steadily and those of the North expanded, not in number, but in the scale and variety of their products. Gradually a new market was developing, the forerunner of the great mass demand of the 19th century, in which the great majority of the population was able to buy glass for the first time. Not surprisingly perhaps, popular taste turned first to coloured glass; and for this demand the factories supplied the wealth of bottles, jugs and bowls, in blue, green, purple, and amethyst, which were chiefly sold at country fairs, up to the 1850's. Together with the still continuing manufacture of green bottle glass, they may be called part of the vernacular tradition.

This demand was met and further enhanced by a whole series of what can only be called glass toys, though they were, and are, colloquially known as 'friggers' by the workmen or gaffers who made them, at first in their spare time, to amuse themselves or their families, and later for

Tankard and bottle with 'speckled' design.
c. 1800. Attributed to Nailsea.
Seddon Collection

Flask with attractive 'swag' design in
white. Early 19th century.
Seddon Collection

commercial production. Brightly coloured, the emphasis indeed being on almost gaudy clashes of colour, and fancifully shaped, these toys represent a silent revolution, the freeing of the imagination of the glass workmen themselves from the canons of classical taste. Most of them are crude, many frankly vulgar or undistinguished, but the best have a native vigour and originality which somehow expresses itself through the form of the glass in a way which had been largely impossible since the introduction of the Excise Tax limited the use of the metal nearly a century before. To a genuine degree, the 'friggers' are a form of popular art, and have been increasingly appreciated as such. They take a bewildering degree of shapes and sizes, defying the cataloguer. Some, like the single or double flasks, in plain or coloured glass or striped work, were made for domestic use, to contain liquids such as oil and vinegar. Others, like the very elaborate hunting scenes, groups of birds, or ships, mounted on a glass sea, and protected beneath a glass dome, must have been made for relatively wealthy customers. The great majority, the pipes, bells, hats, boots, etc., were for amusement and decoration.

The origin of these glass novelties is still a matter of some dispute. In the past they were all lumped together in a general attribution to the factory at Nailsea near Bristol and many collectors and dealers still employ this term. But the history of the Nailsea factory gives very little encouragement to this opinion.

The Nailsea factory is seven miles from Bristol in an area which was making window glass and bottles in the 17th century. In 1788 a Bristol glass-maker, John Robert Lucas, built a glass-house at Nailsea and five years later went into partnership with William Chance, whose family remained associated with the glassworks until its end in 1873. The records show that the great bulk of manufacture in the whole of this period was of crown or window glass and bottle glass. A large amount of domestic ware was made in bottle glass; green jugs, bowls, beakers and flasks, and also friggers like walking sticks, shepherds' crooks, rolling pins, and drumsticks; but certainly nothing in flint, or coloured glass. Perhaps also the popular style of darker green wares were made, flecked with white and other colours, which were characteristic of, among other places, Wrockwardine in Shropshire. But the attribution, in so many collections, of

Right
Bells decorated with wrythen moulding. *c.* 1820.

Next page
Rolling pins with variations in colour design. Early 19th century.
Seddon Collection

Typical examples of 'friggers', the ruler with opaque and coloured spirals. Early 19th century.
Seddon Collection

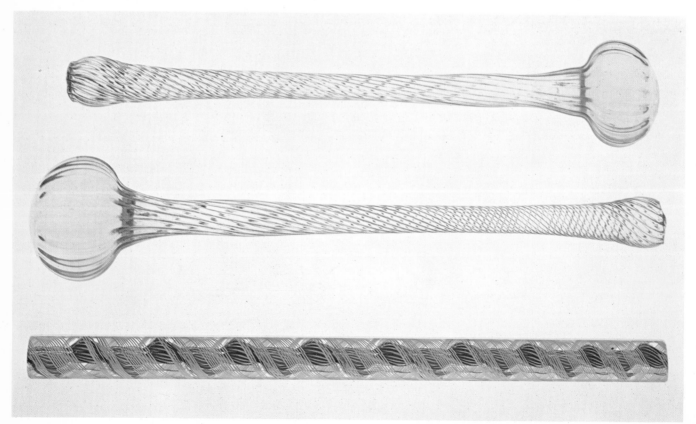

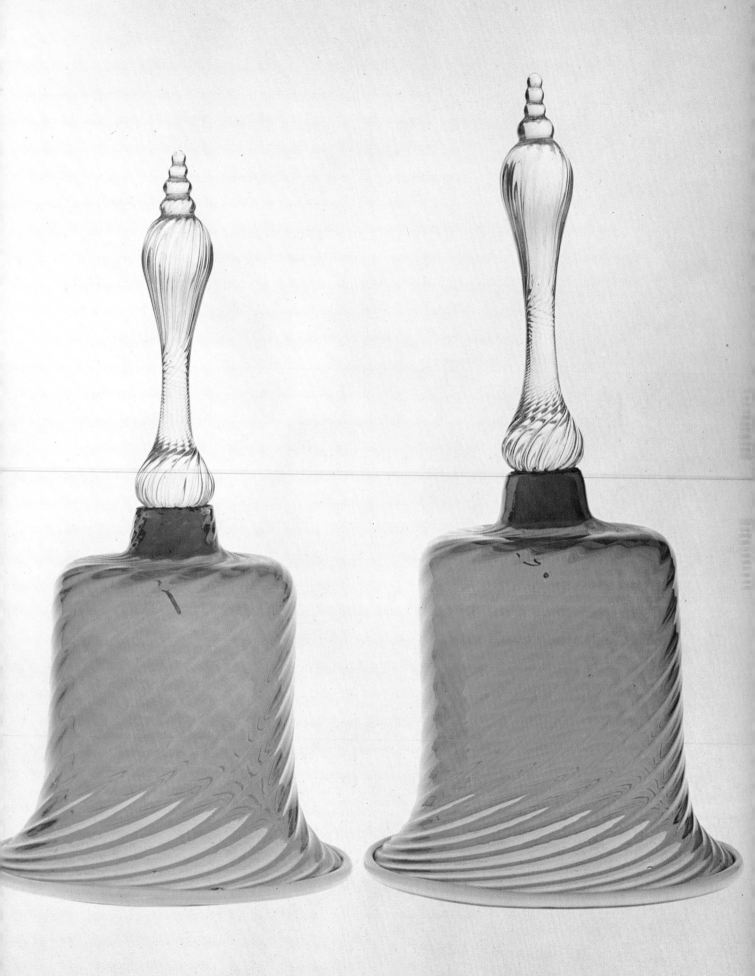

objects of plain or striped coloured glass to Nailsea is incorrect.[1]

For the origin of all these, one must look instead to a far more wide-spread manufacture, chiefly in and around Stourbridge, but including glass-houses all over the Midlands, the North and the Bristol area itself. Five main categories of this type of glass may be listed:

1. Flecked glass, in colour varying from dark green to black—mainly jugs, flasks, bottles, vases.

[1]c.f. Sir Hugh Chance: *Records in the Nailsea Glassworks* (Connoisseur, July, 1967).

Below
Pipe with unusual knop formation. Attributed to Nailsea, early 19th century.
Seddon Collection

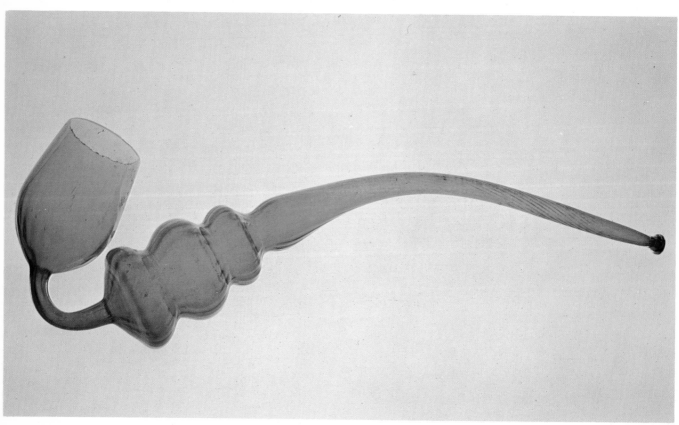

Next page
Pair of candlesticks with unusual combination of colour. Midlands, *c.* 1860.
Seddon Collection

Left
Plain Bristol tankard. *c.* 1790.
Tankard with unusual moulded floral pattern. Early 19th century.
Seddon Collection

Three Bristol pieces illustrating variety of craftsmanship. Boot glasses were made in derision of the Earl of Bute. *c.* 1800.
Seddon Collection

2. Pale green bottles and jugs, sometimes flecked or blotched, sometimes striped with broad bands of red or blue.

3. Pale green (bottle glass) toys and friggers.

4. Flint, opal or coloured glass bells, pipes, flasks; the coloured specimens are either plain or decorated with coloured loops and stripes.

5. Flint or coloured glass toys and friggers.

Only those of the first three categories were made at Nailsea.

How many of the friggers were made for amusement and how many for sale is impossible to determine. It seems that in the Bristol area they were soon exploited by dealers and became for a time staple products. Certainly the same tradition grew up at Stourbridge and may have been taken there by workmen migrating from one factory to another. Elaborate set pieces like the cages of coloured birds, with infinitely fine feather spun tails must have been made to order, for they would have had no place in a workman's cottage. But other amusing objects, such as the whole series of rolling-pins in blue, red or white opaque glass, often painted in unfired oil colours which have worn badly, with inscriptions and mottoes or

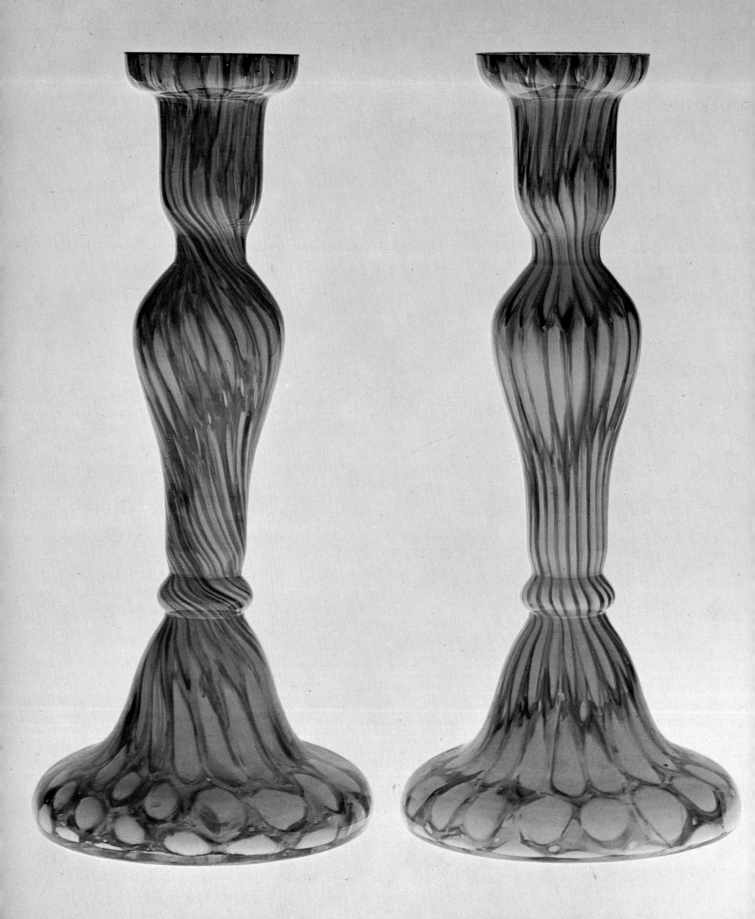

scenes, were intended to be hung as decoration—although the romantic explanation that they were put up in the kitchen while the man of the house was at sea may be discounted for the more prosaic view that they contained tea or sugar.

Apart from the actual domestic glass-ware made for use, the objects most usually found are bells and pipes in shades of pink and blue and striped glass, and walking sticks. Many of the latter have coloured canes inside the stems. The great period of these fancies was the thirty years

81

Vase with colour twist stem and decanter
with white 'speckled' design. Probably
Stourbridge, mid-19th century.
Seddon Collection

Ship in blue and white glass threads, with
lighthouse, in contemporary glass case.
Probably Stourbridge, *c.* 1820. 18 inches.
Messrs. Kaslim & Company

Stourbridge inkwell and paperweight with *millefiore* designs. *c.* 1850.

Seddon Collection

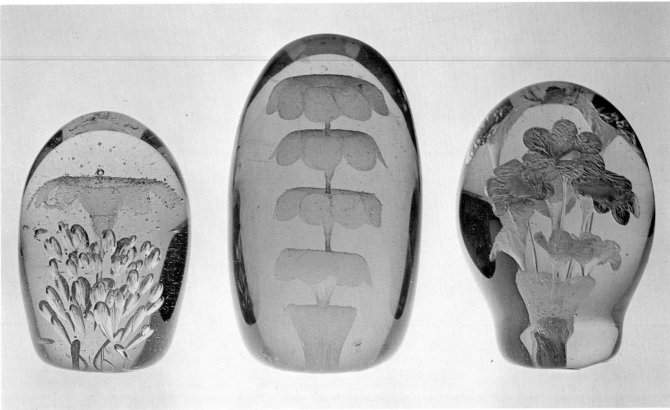

Doorstops showing subject variations. Last quarter of the 19th century.
Seddon Collection

Doorstops with floral motifs. Midlands factories, *c*. 1870.
Seddon Collection

after the Napoleonic Wars. A Newcastle newspaper in 1830 reported a procession of the Guild of Glassmakers through the streets of the city: 'Each wore a hat decorated with a glass feather, a glass star sparkled at their breast, suspended from a chain or collar formed of drops of cut glass in variegated colours hung round the neck. Each man carried a staff, a cross piece at the top displaying a specimen of his art; decanters, goblets, drinking glasses, jugs, bowls, dishes. Some carried a glass bell which he rang lustily.'

Ink bottles with air beaded decoration.
Midlands factories, *c.* 1870.

Seddon Collection

6. Glass Port-raits

James Tassie

Quite unrelated to other late 18th century developments in glass, but again with origins in a more ancient tradition, the manufacture of miniature portraits in white opaque vitreous enamel was carried on by the Tassie brothers. There are obvious ties with the work of miniature painters and later with silhouette cutting, and the glass portraits were normally framed in the same way.

James Tassie was born in Glasgow in 1735. He studied sculpture at the Foulis Academy of Fine Arts and later went to Dublin where, in collaboration with Dr Quin, he discovered the vitreous paste which he then successfully employed in reproductions of antique gems and for the casting of wax portraits, medallions modelled from life. Some of the portraits are modelled with the same white background, others are set in

Pair of Tassie portraits of Louis XVI and Marie Antoinette. Unsigned.
Cecil Davis Limited

plain glass. Three years after his arrival in London in 1766, he was invited by Josiah Wedgwood to produce casts of cameos and intaglios. Wedgwood rather grudgingly referred to Tassie as 'an admirable artist and an honourable man whom it is a credit to emulate although his seals are not so good as mine.'

By 1775 Tassie was well enough established in his own right to produce a catalogue of some 3,106 items. His work caught the attention of Catherine the Great of Russia who, in 1783, commissioned him to produce a complete set of his gems and cameos. The collection was subsequently catalogued by Rudolph Eric Raspe, Professor of Archaeology and Keeper of the Museum of Antiquities at Cassel, who published his monograph in two volumes in 1791.

On the death of James Tassie in 1799, the business passed to his nephew William, who published an enlarged edition of his catalogue in 1816; but the firm could not maintain the standard of the founder, of whom his biographer wrote, 'no medallist has made so extensive and important a contribution to national portraiture as James Tassie.' William Tassie retired from the business in 1840 and left it in the hands of John Wilson.

Many eminent personalities were modelled, statesmen, doctors, politicians, bishops and lawyers; among the most interesting are Admiral Lord Nelson, Adam Smith, the political economist, John Adam, the architect, John Harrison, the horologist and James Tassie himself. Nearly all the portraits were dated and signed with impressed inscriptions, the usual dates being between 1780 and 1790. One example is *W. Tassie. f.* (fecit) *1799.*

Portraits modelled by Tassie. Signed and dated.

Cecil Davis Limited

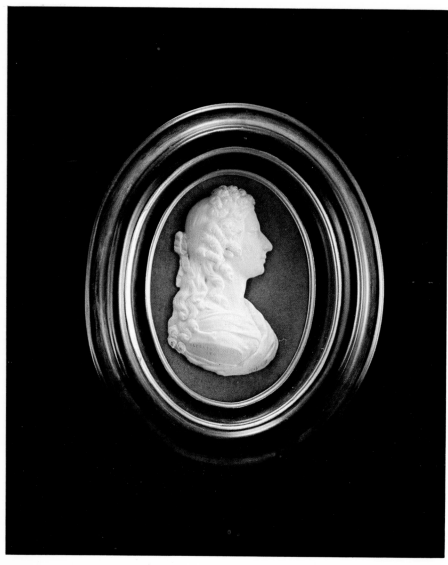

Cameo Encrustation: Apsley Pellatt

Some twenty years after the best of Tassie's work, Apsley Pellatt, owner of the well-known Falcon glass works in Southwark, London, adopted a French invention of imbedding in clear glass small models made from special material. He began to make portrait medallions from a white ceramic paste which would not form gas when heated and which could also expand and contract to the same degree as glass.

Pellatt was to gain a reputation as a glassmaker and inventor and in later life as a politician, but his fame now rests on his portraits set in glass, known as 'sulphides' and 'cameo encrustations', which he himself called 'crystallo-ceramics'. The most attractive feature about the crisp and beautifully clear sulphide technique lies in the blend of the silvery portraits with the heavily cut glass in which they lie. Pellatt applied the process to paperweights, decanters, wine glasses, smelling bottles, jugs, table candelabra and plaques. His best known subjects were portraits of George IV and Queen Caroline on the same scent bottle—possibly sold as coronation souvenirs.

Dating from *circa* 1820, these glass items were fairly heavily cut with designs of diamonds, strawberry diamonds and steps. Now, the rarest examples of the technique are jugs and candelabra. The firm continued in business until at least the middle of the 19th century and at the time of the Great Exhibition in 1851 was making what Pellatt called 'Anglo-Venetian' glass.

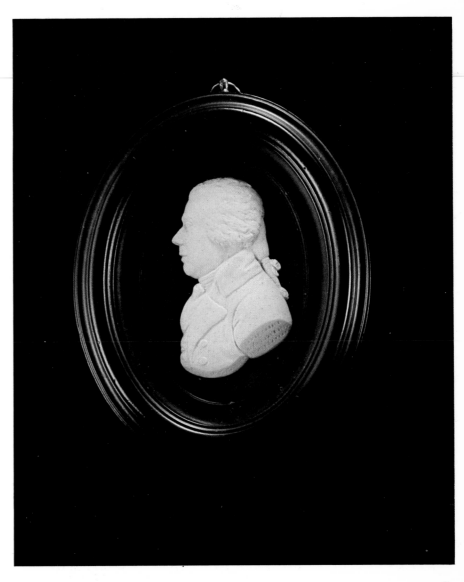

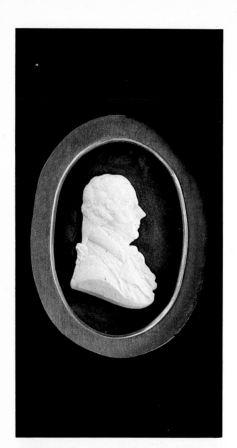

Portraits in vitreous enamel. *Top right* on
a coloured glass ground, date 1809; *top
left*, *below* modelled by Henning, *c.*1800.
Cecil Davis Limited

7. Victorian Coloured Glass

Two 'Richardson, Vitrified Enamel' vases in the classical taste. 12 inches. *c.* 1850.
Godden of Worthing Limited

In the decades after the Napoleonic war, the character of English glass manufacture changed, as its geographical location shifted more and more to the Midlands. The fine glass industry which had grown to its largest

Two 'Richardson, Vitrified Enamel' opaline vases. 8 and 6 inches. *c.* 1850–55.
G. Godden Collection

proportions in London and at Bristol in the West of England as well as the Midlands, became over the period largely concentrated in the smaller Midland triangle of Stourbridge, Birmingham and Dudley. This movement was accompanied by the decline of London, so that by the end of the 19th century the only factory operating there was that of Powell at Whitefriars. Meanwhile in the Midlands, in the production of high class decorative glass, certain firms became supreme, first, through competition with the most elaborate and fanciful products of France and Bohemia in the period

Opaline type vase by Richardson of Stourbridge. Printed mark: 'Richardson, Vitrified Enamel Colours'. 12 inches. *c.* 1850.

G. Godden Collection

up to the Great Exhibition and then, between the 1850's and the end of the century, striking out in forms as characteristically English as those of the great period of lead glass manufacture a hundred and fifty years before. Vastly different though the styles were, there are certain similarities. The best Victorian glass shows an unrestricted use of the metal, in ways more suited to its intrinsic nature than the decoration imposed by foreign influences or the effect of the excise tax, and the full flowering and uninhibited use of colour in and on the material.

Marked ewer: 'Geo. Bacchus & Sons. Vitrified Enamel Colours', in opaline glass. *c.* 1850. 12½ inches.

G. Godden Collection

Undoubtedly the abolition of the glass excise tax in 1845 gave a stimulus to the industry which for a hundred years had complained bitterly that it was faced with ruin. One may doubt that: there was no lack of prosperity in the 18th century and the high level of employment led to fears that the removal of the tax would lead to a shortage of skilled labour; but its abolition coincided with a period of increasing demand for cheap as well as fine glass which laid the economic foundations of the immense prosperity later in the 19th century. After an uneasy time in the 1850's, there followed that golden age of mid-Victorian prosperity—a time of steadily rising wages and standards of living which, despite the setbacks of the 1880's, never really reduced the demand of the middle classes for what had formerly been the prerogatives of the rich and the aristocracy, and of the working class for the things they had never known—glass not only to use but to decorate even the humblest mantelpiece and tables.

Thus in the 19th century, much more than before, the manufacturers were to turn out glass for a variety of markets: the elaborate works shown at the Great Exhibition in 1851 and the vastly expensive cameo carving of the Woodalls and Northwoods were for those who could afford to pay more than £100 for a single ornament; imitations of the fashionable continental designs, overlays, enamelled and painted glass lustres and wildly encrusted centre-pieces were created for the bourgeois who one can recognise so clearly in the novels of Dickens and Galsworthy. Pressed glass, slag glass and the cheap ruby glass were for the artisan who before had known only the crude green bottle and drinking glasses of the vernacular tradition.

The characteristics of the period are themselves bewildering. In the

Richardson frosted glass ewer and goblet, the design registered in April 1847. Ewer 9½ inches.

G. Godden Collection

18th century, changes of fashion had spread to all areas with remarkable similarity and speed. Now a love of novelty for its own sake was combined with a restless search for variety and faster shifts of fashion to produce competition in design, technique and decoration. Between 1837 and 1900 the firm of Thomas Webb evolved over 20,000 patterns and designs and, at the Great Exhibition, Richardsons alone listed 278 items in current production. The overlap of styles and the diversity of objects makes classification and dating, in the 18th century sense, impossible; and one

Right
Table lamp with overlay decoration. *c.* 1860.

Cecil Davis Limited

Pair of marked Richardson vases in imitation of Bohemian coloured glass. 13½ inches. *c.* 1850–55.

Godden of Worthing Limited

must concentrate rather on analysis by styles, types and the factories which produced identifiable work. But behind all the flux of change can be seen a steadily growing love of decoration for its own sake, an abandonment of simplicity for elaboration, rising out of the various revivals of the first half of the 19th century; a love of decoration which above all else manifested itself in the use of colour and for which the manufacturers designed not only new shapes and objects in glass but new colours for the material itself.

The best known of the factories are, in the period before 1851, Davis, Greathead & Green, and W. H. B. & J. Richardson of Stourbridge, Hawkes & Co. of Dudley, and George Bacchus & Sons, Rice Harris & Son, and Lloyd & Summerfield, all of Birmingham. After 1851 the firms of Thomas Webb, Stevens & Williams and Bolton & Mills rose to prominence. But all these are only the famous names among a mass of smaller factories who did not mark their wares, imitating the productions of the best or, like the nothern factories, making their own particular products. Gradually, over the century, a centralising tendency made itself felt and by 1900, in the

face of vastly greater competition, the list of factories had diminished.

One other long term influence should be mentioned: the close connection with American glass-works. The manufacturers of Britain and the United States were far closer in style and technique in the 19th century to each other than they were to those of Europe and there is evidence of considerable interchange of ideas as well as manufactures. Trade between the two countries which, in the early 19th century, was chiefly restricted to American imports of Irish cut glass, increased on both sides and influenced similar developments in each country, as a glance at the United States patterns in Ruth Webb Lee's *Victorian Glass Handbook* will show. Probably the introduction of American press moulding after the 1830's was the most significant innovation but one could also instance the invention of the Burmese shade of colour by the Mount Washington Glass Company of Massachusetts, the cameo work done in the United States by emigrant Stourbridge workmen, and in the 1880's the significant revival of cut glass in the United States which influenced a similar and long term revival in England.

Pair of Mary Gregory vases with enamel figure subjects. *c.* 1870.

Miss H. Morris

The later 19th century can be divided into two periods, roughly either side of 1851. Apart from the Bristol and that commonly, though inaccurately, called Nailsea work and the commercial manufacture of green bottle glass, there was relatively little use of coloured glass before the repeal of the excise tax in 1845, nothing at least to compare with the heavy coloured glass of Bohemia, the overlay work, the hyalith and lithyalin of the Biedermeier age nor the opaline glass of France. In Britain the tradition of clear lead glass, heavily cut in diamond or mitred patterns, was still strong;

Before the Great Exhibition

Below left
Cameo vase, Stevens & Williams. *c.* 1890.
Overlay with cut cameo flowers.

Two Thomas Webb cameo vases in the
Japanese style, having engraved Webb
marks. *c.* 1880. 8 and 7¾ inches.
Private Collection

Below right
Marked vase; 'Thos. Webb & Sons.
Cameo' with patterned ground. *c.* 1885.
8 inches.
Private Collection

Left
Pair of Webb-type cameo-cut vases.
Unmarked, *c.* 1880. 12 inches.
Private Collection

Amethyst scent bottle, probably Bristol
c. 1760. Enamelled, cut and gilt decoration.
Corning Museum of Glass

and such coloured glass as was made in the Midlands followed either the Bristol fashions or attempted to copy Bohemia. Layered or cased glass was being made by Stevens & Hill in the 1840's, 'gold enamel' ware by Thomas Hawkes at Dudley and ruby red stained glass (made with a stain derived from copper) in the Stourbridge area. This latter was normally engraved with simple flower, vine or fruiting patterns.

Stourbridge had been a home of glass manufacturers since the early 17th century but until the 19th its glass works had followed the usual trends. However, the work exhibited by Benjamin Richardson at the Manchester Exhibition of 1845 in opaline glass, layered and painted work showed that the situation had changed and that a serious attempt was being made to compete with foreign importation. Four years later, at the Birmingham Exhibition, coloured and opaline glass formed the major part of the exhibits; and the firms now included Bacchus, Rice Harris and Lloyd Summerfield. This tendency reached its peak in the manufactures shown at the Great Exhibition of 1851. Because most of this work was imitative of the Continent, classification is not easy, and it would not be

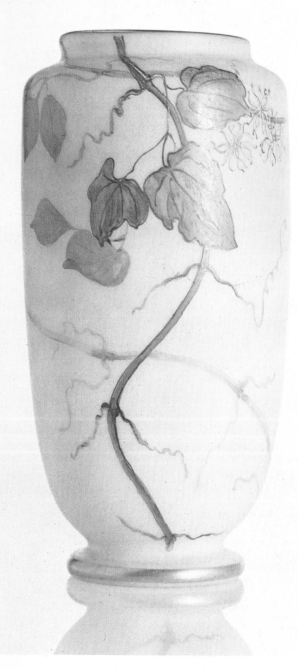

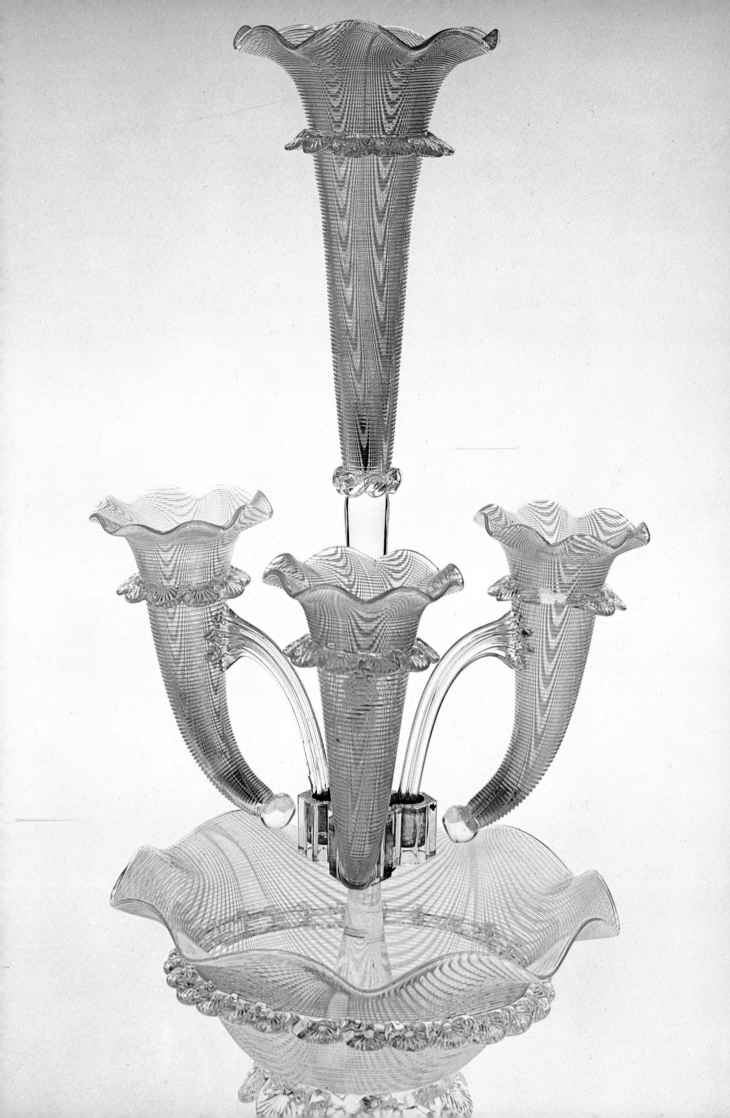

too harsh to say that the majority of British work was still well behind the techniques of Bohemia, although its greater simplicity and lightness make it perhaps more attractive to the modern taste. The principle types of manufacture in this period are as follows:

Plain Coloured Glass. Mainly used for bottles, toilet sets, sets of wine glasses, usually cut with flat broad flutes. The colours range from the so-called Bristol blues, purples and greens to ruby, amber and pale green.

Ornate Stourbridge glass bowl with applied mouldings. *c.* 1885. 7 inches.
G. Godden Collection

The blue colour of Bristol glass, which had become paler during the period of the Napoleonic wars when supplies of cobalt were cut off, returned after 1820 to the more popular deep purple. Much of the glass made in shades of blue and green which continued in production into the present century is often called Bristol; in general the early and mid 19th century blue and green glass was cut with broad flutes and is to be found especially in decanters and sets of wine glasses with bucket bowls. Blue water jugs and sets of wine glasses, and goblets with double ogee shaped

Stourbridge cream jug and basin with applied decoration. *c*. 1880.

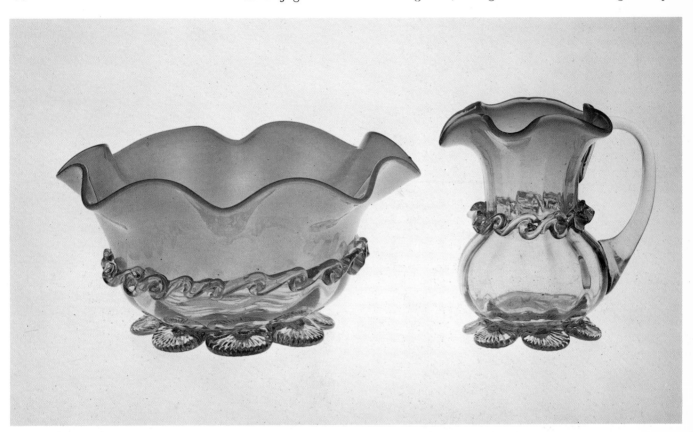

bowls are much later, and red glasses and decanters are almost certainly Continental imports.

The little coloured jugs, mugs and creamers which are associated with Bristol and Nailsea at the end of the 18th century continued until about the 1840's when they were killed off by the introduction of cheaper pressed glass. Mostly made to be sold at country fairs, they followed closely the design of Staffordshire pottery and there were still gilded mottoes on blue and purple glass such as 'Be canny with the cream', in rough gilding or enamelling which has usually worn badly over the years.

Layered (Cased or Overlay) Glass. The English factories produced a somewhat different response to the Bohemian models, sensitive to the current fashion for the Gothic taste. Layered glass was made by encasing the original glass vessel in one or more layers of glass of a different colour and then cutting through the layers to reveal patterns in the colours beneath. Most of the better pieces were then decorated with gilding and enamel, with sprigs of flowers, portraits or domestic scenes. The colours used might be opaque white on clear glass, or a variety of contrasting colours often with white in between to distinguish them. The cutting was usually flat, in broad facets, often with Gothic shapes like church windows, though occasionally mitre cutting was used. The majority of pieces were vases or lustres (vase or candlestick shaped ornaments, hung with long clear glass drops), usually made in pairs, whose obvious function was to stand on mantelpieces. On a number of specimens the motif of leaves, flowers or trailing vines is also cut through the casing. These are usually in ruby on a clear base. This whole fashion continued well into the second half of the 19th century but since no English specimens are marked, it becomes a matter largely of

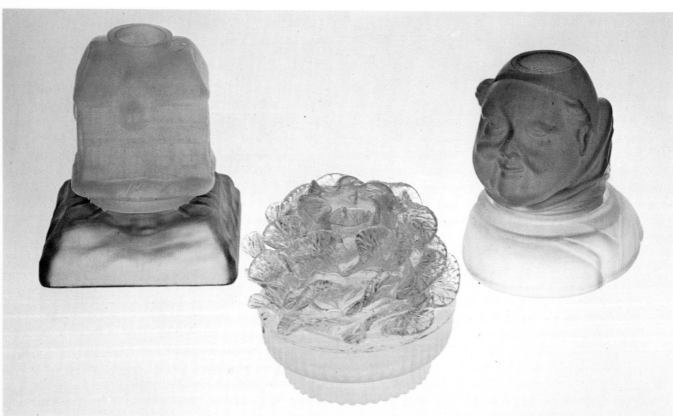

speculation to decide their country of origin.

Flashed Glass. An inferior form of the above made more simply by allowing the original glass base vessel to cool and then merely dipping it in molten coloured glass rather than encasing it properly. The film thus produced was much thinner and the cutting flatter. In general this work was done with clear glass dipped in ruby, amethyst, amber or green and then decorated with acid etching, or a simple cut design.

Above
Group of night or 'Fairy' lamps as produced in Stourbridge for Samuel Clarke. *c.* 1885–90.
Godden of Worthing Limited

Below
Three fancy night or 'Fairy' lamps, examples of several novelties in this line. *c.* 1890. The rose, 3½ inches.
Godden of Worthing Limited

Two novelty night or 'Fairy' lamps, an Indian elephant and Queen Victoria. *c.* 1890.

Seddon Collection

Bowl with mother of pearl finish. *c.*1885. In an American stand.

Satin glass bowl, probably English, *c.* 1885. In an American stand.

Corning Museum

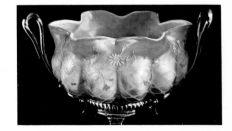

Opaline Glass. Although British factories again imitated those of Europe their products were differentiated in both form and decoration. Probably the tradition of Bristol opaque glass never died out; but the 18th century shapes changed to those common to both porcelain and glass in the mid 19th century. Opaline, in spite of the warm vermilion colour which it reveals when held against a light, does not reflect, and it was best used, like porcelain, for its shape and the surface which it offered to the decorator. A speciality of the Richardson factory was two-coloured opaline and

occasionally parts of opaline jugs and vases are found with diamond or mitre cutting; but the most common form of working the surface was to roughen it to contrast with the polished surface of the painting or transfer prints on the body. Many of the Stourbridge pieces were made with flared rims, edged in green enamel or moulded in the form of applied snakes and reptiles.

The painted decoration falls into many categories, some of which are illustrated here. On marked specimens, Bacchus tended towards painting in panels of flowers, while Richardson developed a whole variety of scenes. The Richardson pieces are decorated over the whole surface, the flowers rising from the base in naturalistic groups, with swags and tendrils and fine gilding at the bases and tops. Other designs grew out of the many revivals of classical fashion, the Greek, Egyptian, and Etruscan motifs of the 1840's and 50's. A whole series of groups of classical figures surrounded by friezes were made, some marked, a great majority unmarked, by glasshouses all over the Midlands. Indian and Chinese scenes were popular and gilding was often added to the formal framework of the design. Other

Previous page
Group of glass flowers. *c.* 1880.

Seddon Collection

Sowerby 'Ivory' pressed-glass candlestick (10½ inches) and oval basket of design registered in February 1879. Relief moulded crest marks.

G. Godden Collection

Small Sowerby pressed-glass basket trinket, design registered in May 1878. Relief moulded crest mark. 3 inches.
G. Godden Collection

Pair of 'slag-glass' saltcellars, bearing the relief moulded crest mark of George Davidson & Co. of Gateshead-on-Tyne. *c.* 1880. 2½ inches.
G. Godden Collection

factories which marked their wares were Rice Harris, and the decorator J. F. Christy of Lambeth. An attractive series of opaline decanters was also made, in tall thin shapes with wine or spirit labels reminiscent of the engraved labels of the 1740's.

Not all opaline glass was painted and there was a demand for cheaper pieces which was met by the use of transfer printing. Again, classical and oriental scenes and friezes were employed: the whole style of decoration implies the return to ancient models, familiar in architecture and sculpture as well as porcelain at the time. But from the amateur and naturalistic character of many of the paintings it must be presumed that opaline vases were frequently bought in the plain state and decorated at home: no doubt a suitable subject matter for many of the talented Victorian women of the day.

Painting on Clear Glass. The advantage of enamelling clear glass was that any liquid inside could be seen, and whereas the painted opaline vessels are obviously ornamental, the clear glass ones were mostly for use. Richardson produced wine glasses, decanters and jugs, and there are a host of decanters, bottles and tumblers painted with flowers which are very difficult to distinguish from contemporary Continental types. The best English glass in this category was decorated by the firm of J. F. Christy and the styles were much imitated even after the firm went out of business in the early 1850's. They commissioned from Richard Redgrave, the artist, the design of the 'water plant' which they used on decanters and jugs; but painting of this standard was rare.

Painting on Coloured Glass. Sometimes this painting is associated with Thomas Bott, but this is unlikely, as he worked nearly all his life for the Worcester porcelain factory. Most of the painting on coloured glass is of rustic scenes and figures in Victorian dress, usually on dark blue and red glass, with added gilding. The gilding is often elaborate and reminiscent more of that contemporary Sèvres porcelain than the restrained patterns of earlier Bristol.

Mary Gregory. Although this term belongs to the period after 1851, it may perhaps be mentioned here. It has been used to describe a genre of paintings of children in Victorian dress in white enamels on late 19th century clear and coloured glass. It is by no means certain that Mary Gregory herself even existed, although it is often said that she worked for the Boston and Sandwich Glass factory in the United States and that her style was modelled on imported Bohemian work. Large quantities of this glass were also exported to England and there is no evidence of the production of anything of similar quality here. Later still in the century a mass of cheaper imitations were produced in crude colours with flesh tints instead of white, normally on clear glass. They can scarcely be compared with either the Bohemian of 'Mary Gregory' work and are not identifiable with any particular factory or region.

Novelties. While the toys and fairings of Nailsea type continued to be made right through this period, and while the glass blowers continued to make their 'friggers', the 1840's brought a number of innovations to coloured glass.

Silvered Glass. Chiefly associated with the Powell factory at Whitefriars, silvered glass was made and shaped like a vacuum flask with double walls, silvered on the inside. A patent was registered in 1849 but the difficulties of manufacture prevented the blowing of elegant shapes and the rather dumpy glasses and bowls remained merely novelties.

Paper Weights. After the remarkable outburst of activity in France in 1845 at Clichy, St. Louis and Baccarat, English manufacturers attempted to match the *millefiori* design of coloured canes inside a circular mass of clear glass, though rarely so ambitious as to include the flowers and snakes of the rarest French designs. Most of the English ones were made in the Midlands and Bacchus were first in the field, exhibiting several designs at Birmingham in 1849. Rice Harris followed shortly after and several of their weights carried the letters I.G.W. (Islington Glass Works). Powell of Whitefriars made portrait weights in the manner of Apsley Pellatt and although these factories were able to compare with the French in quality, the greater number which are associated with Stourbridge are cruder and larger and confined to the simpler *millefiori* pattern.

Manufacturers also turned their hands to inkwells which had the canes in the base and in the stopper, and door knobs. Production continued almost to the end of the 19th century and was followed, for a much cheaper mass market in the second half of the century, by a very large manufacture of green glass weights for use either as paper weights or door stops. These are associated with Yorkshire and other Northern factories. Crude and full of air bubbles, these have a charm of their own: the ordinary examples enclose air in the form of rough flowers but some have animals and birds, often brightly coloured, and one enclosing a ceramic bust of Queen Victoria was made at Nottingly in Yorkshire in

George Davidson & Co. moulded 'slag-glass', bearing the relief moulded lion crest mark. *c.* 1880. Bowl, 5 inches.

G. Godden Collection

1887. Having a vitality of their own, more attractive than the imitations of the French, they form a subject for collecting in themselves.

1851: the Great Exhibition

As in so many other fields, the Great Exhibition proved to be the climax of the period of rapidly changing revivals, the Greek, Etruscan, Mediaeval or Tudor, whose full exuberance fortunately had passed the glass industry by. The key-note of this earlier period was its derivative nature: the best known techniques, layered and stained glass and the opalines, were derived from the Continent; and the majority of designers sought inspiration in antiquity. After the 1850's, design and technique grew so that in the 80's there was a greater gulf between Britain and the Continent than had existed since the end of the 18th century.

The glass wares of the Great Exhibition were more remarkable for their diversity than their native ingenuity, although some hope of distinction could be seen in the work of Richardson (whose prize medal, however, was won for 'cut crystal, opal vases painted with enamelled colours, the Judgement of Paris, the Dream of Penelope, Aesop's Fables, etc. Opal glass ornamented with pet fauns in enamelled colours, Grecian figures in coloured enamels'—designs which so attracted Queen Victoria that she ordered a glass 'with a Venetian foot' for Buckingham Palace). The Exhibition proved the last flowering of the factory of Davis, Greathead & Green of Stourbridge who, though they won no medal, gained the greatest praise of contemporaries. Rice Harris had the longest list of colours 'opal, alabaster, turquoise, amber, canary, topaz, chrysoprase, pink, blue, light and dark ruby, black, brown, green, purple, etc.' Indeed coloured glass for the first time publicly challenged the pre-eminence of English clear glass and this is probably the most significant aspect of the early 1850's. It was as well; for the time was an unsettled one in the glass making industry. New firms like Thomas Webb, who had barely exhibited in 1851, were rising but there seems to have been a shift of fashion against the Continental forms, not entirely dissociated from the political storms of 1848; and the growth of the mass market for plain and coloured glass in sets had not yet provided the secure economic base on which the industry could expand.

By the 1860's, with design and decoration responsive again to the public taste, and with the industry based securely, the picture was very different. There followed the apex of Victorian taste: the glass painters abandoned revivals and replaced them by recognisable English and Scottish scenes, by figures in contemporary dress, naturalistic animals, hunting and shooting scenes. Plain coloured glass superseded clear glass with alarming speed in a revolution which brought sets of amber, amethyst, blue and green wine glasses and decanters, whether blown, moulded or pressed, to the table and also provided the ultimate characteristic of the period—the coloured glass centrepiece. To what remained of clear glass in the hand-made market, the gaffers added a fantastic array of clear and coloured applied decoration, drops and knops, all in wild and often fantastic shapes in a riot of apparently disordered imagination, which can be recognised also in porcelain and furniture, though because of the less plastic nature of these media, to a lesser degree. The period from the 1850's to the 1890's is the most difficult to classify and is best approached through analysis of styles and techniques, rather than a chronology which would be misleading.

Influences

While this was pre-eminently a period of English design, when faster communications were breaking down patterns of trade, Britain was still open to foreign influence. Apsley Pellatt had published in 1849 his *Curiosities of Glassmaking* which described Venetian techniques; and his firm then developed the 'ice glass' or frosted glass which he called Anglo-Venetian. Venetian influence remained slight until the 1860's; but after the Paris Exhibition of 1867, at which Antonio Salviati took pride of place with his revival of the great age of Venice, the influence became stronger, specifically in latticino work and the use of coloured canes and in the techniques of furnace manipulation of clear and coloured applied ornament, and of the stems of wine glasses.

Of lesser importance, because the spirit of Venice was in a sense embodied in much late Victorian, glass work, were the Chinese and Japanese influences in decoration. Western awareness of the art of Japan was new and it can be seen in the applied work on bowls and vases, reminiscent of jade and soapstone carving, by Webb and Stevens & Williams when John Northwood was a member of the firm. There was also a degree of direct French influence: the painting and gilding done for Webb by the workshop of Jules Barbe, a good deal of which was executed on Burmese ware, and by Erard of Stevens & Williams; it can also be seen in the introduction of new metals such as the so called 'moss agate' glass, which gave a body of streaked and crackled appearance not unlike Blue John or fluorspar.

Etching. Etching by acid was a simple process in use early in the 19th century and certainly employed by Thomas Hawkes of Dudley from the 1830's. The process involves covering the glass surface with a wax or other substance which resists acid, then scratching or cutting it away to make the pattern. The vessel is dipped in acid for the required time, then removed and cleaned to reveal the pattern which has been eaten away. Differing lengths of time allow for different depths of etching. Mainly used on plain glass, etching was employed by Richardson on coloured glasses in the late 1850's. Soon after, John Northwood and Thomas Guest established firms specialising in acid engraving. In the 1880's acid was used to produce what was called 'satin finish', often in conjunction with patterns made up from trapped air between an opaque body and a tinted overlay with a satin finish.

Carving. The most spectacular development of the period was the delicate and immensely lengthy work of cameo carving on glass. It was first inspired by the discovery that the famous Roman Portland vase, so often imitated by Wedgwood, was actually made of glass. The body had been overlaid with an opaque white case which had been cut away by hand to reveal the deep blue beneath in marvellously moulded classical figures. John Northwood was the pioneer of this technique and after he had carved the clear Elgin vase which, strictly speaking, is intaglio work, he was commissioned to make a copy of the Portland vase. After initial failures, caused by the difficulty of the annealing process of fitting the body to the overlay, he succeeded and other splendid and unique pieces followed. All were highly expensive—the Portland vase cost £1,000 and even when the technique was learnt and used on lesser but still fine pieces, they were costly. Northwood himself set up as a manufacturer with Stevens & Williams; Thomas Webb followed, for whom worked the indefatigable brothers George and Tom Woodall (nephews of Thomas Bott); also Richardson, who employed A. E. Lecheveral, a Frenchman, and Joseph Locke, who later emigrated to the United States to the Guest factory.

The 1880's saw the peak of cameo carving. Soon the immensely laborious work of carving was speeded up by the use of the engraving wheel. This first stage of commercial production retained the spirit of the art, while departing from the strict classical fashion. Chiefly prized today are the plaques by the Woodall brothers in the pre-Raphaelite style, which command immense prices. Somewhat more modest were the vases and urns with flower rather than figure subjects, which are of remarkable beauty; but cameo carving was for a small and wealthy market, an entirely English one, the only Continental equivalent being the vastly different style of Emile Gallé in France.

In about 1900 the art began to die. The introduction of imitations made by using a thinner overlay and cutting it away with acid or simply by painting on the design and firing it, led to a flooding of the market

New Techniques

just when the demand itself began to fall off. Large quantities of these later imitations exist; the overlay is thin and often of poor quality but the designs, copying those of the 1880's and '90's and incorporating Art Nouveau remain attractive, at least up to the first World War, and they are not without appeal to collectors. These are seldom marked; the better cameos almost invariably were signed.

Applied Decoration. Beginning with clear glass and then, after 1870, in more and more extravagant colours, applied decoration of almost every imaginable variety was introduced, often without any thought for the intrinsic use of the object itself. Fantastic exercises in decoration led to wildness, even incoherence of shapes, rustic additions, flowing and coiled snakes, and other animals and asymmetrical forms which by the end of the century lead into something recognisable as an English Art Nouveau. Drawing on the imagination of the gaffers and the long tradition of friggers, the bowls and vases, jugs and flower holders take on as many forms as the whims of the glass maker: prunts and globules like raindrops, plain or coloured, beads and trails, twigs, flowers and branches, ribbing, scroll legs, rustic feet, pincered work, frills in the necks of vessels, and close twisted rope handles (unlike the looser twists of the early 19th century). The only category that can be defined is that of certain regular patterns in use at the Stourbridge factories: the acanthus leaf, the Japanese style of branches and flowers trailed round the body of the glass and the sprays of blackthorn and English flowers.

Silvered Glass. Made by depositing a layer of silver on the glass—giving the impression of a fine mesh-like filigree. This development is associated with Stevens & Williams in the 1870's.

Latticino. The use of opaque white and coloured enamel in the body of the glass vessel was common in the period before the Great Exhibition and can partly be distinguished from the so-called Nailsea work by a closer resemblance to the Venetian, both in delicacy of the latticino threads and in the actual shapes of glasses or vessels. The patterns of this period tend to extreme simplicity; a few threads in panels and twists rising at the side of the bowl and the use of coloured canes in the stem which, though more than the colour twists of the 18th century, is still sparing. Pellatt, Bacchus and Richardson all worked in this fashion.

In the 1880's the style revived, apparently at the same time as a fall in demand for glass with raised decoration; and the fashion was led by the workshop of John Northwood. The method known as 'pull up' threading was to insert the coloured enamels in the base and draw them up through the body of the glass with a pointed iron hook, making the pattern on the way. It was difficult and Northwood invented a pull-up machine—a spindle with fixed and movable metal arms which could be manipulated to form patterns of greater intricacy and regularity. Herringbone and parabolic designs were made possible over the whole surface of the glass and were followed by heavier and more elaborate work. More canes were used in the stems of glasses and a greater variety of colours overall: white, pink, yellow, blue and various mixtures, while a style grew up in which bands of latticino work alternated with bands of coloured blobs. One of Northwood's patterns was of vertical bands of trapped air bubbles on a ribbed body called the 'Jewell' pattern. A further development of the method led to a variation in layered glass in which the overlay trapped air in threaded and moulded patterns.

New Colours. In the fiercely competitive atmosphere of the late 19th century, in which the United States as well as British factories were involved, manufacturers explored the creation of new colours in glass itself. The most famous of these, 'Queen's Burmese Ware', with its iridescent shades moving from creamy yellow to subtle red, was in fact the invention of the Mount Washington Glass Company of Massachusetts, but Thomas Webb followed closely after; in successive years they introduced, Bronze (1878), Peach (1885), Burmese (1886), Old Roman (1888), and Tricolour (1889). Since the iridescent shades were best seen when well lit or lit from behind, they were employed in centre-pieces, candle shades, screens and fairy lights. A whole literature has grown up around the latter genre: the best of them, even in the 1880's costing five shillings, were made in these elaborate colours or in the latticino style, while cheaper varieties—all in the Webb's advertisements—descended to press moulded lights in plain colours costing one shilling a dozen. But the rate of breakage was high, particularly if the night-lights inside were not properly fixed, and they have become collectable objects with a large vogue in the United States. They can be found in the forms of cottages, comic figures and other toys.

Centre-pieces. While the fairy lights could be called new objects, the most striking and characteristic phenomenon of the period was the evolution of the centre-piece. In the 18th century there had been glass centre decorations, usually for households which could not afford the same in silver: candelabra, épergnes, bonbon dishes, and so on. These things continued to be made during the early 19th century in heavily cut glass. But there is no real precursor to the centre-piece which developed in the 1860's and lasted till after 1900; because the primary function was now less for use than as sheer decoration—what would now be called a status symbol. The centre-pieces expressed at once the sense of prosperity, ostentation and pride of bourgeois England and the fantasy which lay behind it. Whether posing as holders for sweets, festooned with little baskets, or as flower stands with trumpet shaped holders, as épergnes or plateaux (with mirror bases) or as candelabra, they were intended as ornaments in themselves for the table. Some, as a *reductio ad absurdum*, were made to sit for ever under the domed glass cases familiar to the period and these, in which the coloured glass was often mounted in garishly moulded silver plate, probably rested in the centre of the mantelpiece.

London firms took a leading part in their production. Many of the designs of the 1860's were registered by Daniel Pearce (of the firm of Dobson and Pearce) who later joined Webb and carried on with this work through the 1880's. Other firms associated with flower holders were Naylor & Co. of London, Bolton and Mills of Stourbridge, and Richardson; with basket holders, James Green, Powell & Richardson; and one branch of manufacturing included chandeliers of similar colours and designs to the contemporary Venetian of the 1870's. Whether made with basket holders or for flowers, the most usual design is that of a tall central column rising directly from the base, with three smaller stems fitted into a metal collar part of the way up the parent stem. Leaves in many shapes were often inserted between the subsidiary stems, as they were in the chandeliers. Most centre-pieces stand at least one foot high and the largest are over two feet. Colours include all varieties from clear glass to Burmese and the flower holders were made of latticino work as well as encrusted and applied designs. Centre-pieces were a popular export to the United States but their production fell off in the 1890's. They seem to have been overtaken, partly by a different type of flower holder made up of a number of smaller holders in the form of tree trunks, roots or branches. Richardson's made these in hollow bamboo designs and J. W. Walsh in the form of foxglove flowers. In their rustic and asymmetrical design, the flower holders are nearer to the flowing shapes of Art Nouveau than the rigid high Victorian centre-pieces which had virtually ceased to be made before the first World War.

Almost as characteristic of the period, though made with less extravagance of design, were the lustres which were inseparable from the Victorian mantelpiece. Originally made in imitation of Bohemian overlay, by the later 19th century these were made in plain colours, chiefly blue, and in opaline, and were decorated with flower painting or gilding. For all their resemblance to candlesticks, they had no practical use. The great majority are hung with the type of drops known as 'Alberts': triangular in section with a head like an arrow and scalloped cutting on the edges.

The Arts and Crafts Movement. The movement associated with William Morris which involved, for the decorative arts, the idea of returning to hand craftsmanship and the setting of painstaking art against the soulless machine, affected glass manufacture. The first conscious work which can be associated with these ideas was a series of glasses designed by Philip Webb for William Morris in 1860; ten years later a whole genre could be ascribed to the influence of the 'Arts and Crafts' movement. James Powell & Son, who made the glasses for Morris at their Whitefriars factory, continued to design consciously purist glasses: sometimes in colour, sometimes plain, but in their simplicity and occasional hankerings after mediaeval forms quite apart from the luxuriance of high Victorian designs. They were no doubt influenced by Ruskin, who thought glass a fluid substance, not to be carved deeply like stone, but to have its true nature wrought from the form of the metal itself. The work was presumably kept alive by the demands of a small group of *cognoscenti*, and Powell's were, in the late 19th century, the only firm in London making hand-made glass. Their most characteristic technique was the use of furnace manipulation of the stems and bodies of pale coloured or opalescent glass, with decoration adapted from early and delicate Venetian forms of the 16th and 17th centuries. Probably they were making the best and most advanced glass in Britain; certainly in 1900 the glasses which they exhibited in Paris, of slender plastic shapes chastely ornamented with latticino work, were excellent examples, comparable with anything in Europe.

This whole subject is, as yet, little charted and is usually listed under the general heading of Whitefriars, but A. Jenkinson of Edinburgh was making beautifully thin and delicate 'muslin' glass, which he exhibited at Paris as early as 1878, and in another direction altogether, James Couper & Sons of Glasgow went in for a purist type called 'Clutha' glass—pale green, streaked and bubbled like Roman glass, in forms of great simplicity, devised by Christopher Dresser, one of the forerunners of Art Nouveau.

Scotland was indeed one of the most progressive areas, possibly helped by the rich and discriminating, as well as locally patriotic, citizens of Glasgow and Edinburgh. Couper & Sons produced a second series of Clutha designs by George Walton; and the Glasgow style associated with C. R. Macintosh and Herbert McNair influenced the manufacture of stained glass windows and table glass in designs remarkably like those of Aubrey Beardsley. This Celtic revival, interspersed with the influence of Japan, and the influence of the Arts and Crafts movement, represents, in the decorative arts, the British Art Nouveau. There was no sharp break, as on the Continent, and indeed the Continental style owed much to British developments in the period 1860–90. It was the wave of criticism which followed, which prevented a full development of the new style in glass, as well as other fields.

The Midlands, previously so much in the fore-front of Victorian fashion, lagged behind. Stourbridge was preoccupied in the late 1890's and early 1900's with a return to the older and now wholly commercialised production of cased glass, heavily cut clear glass and elaborate engraving.

Meanwhile an entirely new market had grown up outside the hand-made glass which we have been discussing in the rest of this chapter. Working class families might possibly aspire to a centre-piece in the 1870's—but for actual domestic use and for most of the decoration of their houses, they turned to the cheap machine-made products and mechanical reproductions of hand-made articles. The great mass-producing area was of course the Midlands, on a rather wider scale than Stourbridge itself, and this market was the bread and butter of firms whose names were never impressed on their wares and who rarely even bothered with elaborate trade catalogues.

In this category lies the cheap blown or moulded ruby glass with crude decoration applied in clear glass; the material is poor and the styles altered little from the 1860's when the moulds were made. Most of the glass produced by small cribs in the Midlands was remelted from the waste of other factories and the only distinctive wares which should be mentioned are the friggers with which the glass workers amused themselves, or which they perhaps made for sale in local and country markets. Generally ten or twenty years behind the fashion, this category of ruby glass is unlikely ever to become collectable because of its immense quantity, poor quality and lack of variety; but the friggers should, for they have the same attributes as the toys usually associated with Nailsea and a genuinely vernacular tradition of craftsmanship. Pigs, cows, horses, fish, birds, pipes, hats, caps, firemen's helmets, walking-sticks, huntsmen, ships, eggs (hand coolers), boots, shoes, slippers, inkwells, umbrellas, nursery tea sets, in clear glass, opaline, blue, latticino, orange, red, and green, the list is endless. Many of them are almost indistinguishable from the early 19th century pieces and are, in fact, probably part of the continuing tradition reflecting only the geographical move of the workmen from the West Country to the Midlands within the industry itself.

Mechanical Glassmaking. By far the greatest demand for glass was, of course, purely mechanical: window glass which had, by its nature, to be clear, and bottle glass which, since it was cheaper, continued through much of the 19th century to be made of pale or dark green metal. But mechanical means could also be used to produce cheap decorative glassware and manufacturers were not slow to take advantage of the chance. Decanters had been blown into moulds since the 18th century and the 'blown three mould' method was widely used in the United States in the early 19th century. Although in operation in Britain commercially at the same time, mould blowing was little used for decorative wares and certainly not for mass production. Apsley Pellatt manufactured a certain amount of 'pillar' moulded objects (with heavy blown pillars formed round the outside of the body). However, in the mid and late 19th century, moulding was largely employed by firms like Stevens & Williams in their 'utility trade' of glassware for hotels, railways and public authorities.

Press Moulding. Press moulding came in from the United States in the 1820's and 30's, although it had, again, been used in England in the 18th century, as in the press moulded square bases of many English and Irish glasses. It was rapidly developed, chiefly to reproduce and copy the finer cut glass, and the manufacture was carried on especially in the Midlands until the eclipse of the fashion for cut glass around the 1860's. At this stage the manufacturers of pressed glass were unwilling to give up a profitable mass market in tableware just at the moment when the great Victorian development of retail and distributive trades was beginning, and they turned to differences of texture and then to the use of colour. The period of press moulding, which runs to the end of the century, was chiefly associated with the Northern glass works: Henry Greener of Sunderland, Sowerby's Ellison Glass Works and George Davidson, both of Gateshead, W. H. Heppell of Newcastle, Butler, Tate & Co. of Manchester, and John Ford of Edinburgh; although this list may merely reflect the fact that only these factories impressed their mark or registration date mark on the base. The mark of Sowerby's is a peacock's head; the others can usually be identified and dated by the registration mark.

Slag glass, as it has come to be known, from the derivation of the material (silicate slag skimmed off molten steel and then mixed with the clear glass), is now collectable in its own right, the marked pieces being most eagerly sought after. Although some of the pieces were made in plain opaque colours, white, cream, primrose and blue, the main attraction of slag glass is the rich marbled effect obtained in blues, turquoise, oranges, browns, purples and even near black. Because the moulds of slag glass pieces rarely changed, the styles remained the same over the thirty years in which it was at the height of its popularity. The larger objects, the jugs, vases, cake stands, celery vases, particularly those of the Sowerby factory, are elaborate and often adventurous in design; for example, the well-known mould of a water jug in the shape of a fish with its mouth wide open; these pieces are covered with motifs of animals, birds and flowers or figures and are now difficult to find. The more ordinary wares illustrated here cover a wide range of uses from salt cellars to candlesticks, from bowls to tumblers; probably the largest number of pieces are in the form of little baskets, and basket work and diamond cutting was the most common relief pattern. In the 1890's the revival of demand for clear cut glass stimulated a return to straightforward imitations in pressed glass, and slag ware dropped almost wholly out of fashion.

It is still difficult to evaluate the merits of English coloured glass in the late 19th century. Possibly the whole laborious expensive cameo work, the top flight of expensive handicraft, should be written down in artistic terms but its rarity and value in money terms will no doubt preserve it. Certainly the lesser productions, the simpler flowered cameos, of the Webbs and Richardsons, have greater intrinsic appeal today. The glass of the Arts and Crafts movement should, and no doubt will, be recognised as being as worthy as anything in Europe, while the imitations of Continental overlaid and opaline glass remain undistinguished. The mood of elaboration, of sheer exuberant decorativeness, is already returning and may bring with it a revival of high Victoriana.

After 1900 new factors contributed to the decline of the English industry: still cheaper competition from abroad, the pressures of war in 1914, and the Government diversion of glass output for Service requirements. The gaffers and other skilled craftsmen, who were the backbone of the industry, died off and were not replaced by younger men. But perhaps the decisive factor occurred before the war when the public turned, apparently in an irrevocable manner, to the permanent demand for cut glass—for brilliant cutting, making a glass full of artificial fire. This removed, except for a small, largely experimental section, of the glassmaking industry, the use of colour and form, and restricted 20th century English glass to a tradition based largely on the past.